ADOPTION *ADVENTURE*
travel guide

Tales & tips from an adoptive momma

HOLLY NICOLE JAMES

Published in Houston, Texas, by The Mom in Stilettos Publishing, an imprint of The Mom in Stilettos.

All Scripture quotations, unless otherwise indicated, are taken from the Holy Bible, New International Reader's Version®, NIrV® Copyright © 1995, 1996, 1998, 2014 by Biblica, Inc.™ Used by permission of Zondervan. All rights reserved worldwide. www.zondervan.com The "NIrV" and "New International Reader's Version" are trademarks registered in the United States Patent and Trademark Office by Biblica, Inc.™

ISBN: 978-0-692-90626-2 (Paperback)

Printed in the United States of America

the mom in
publishing

For my husband, who is the most loving, patient, and encouraging person. Without you and your dream, none of this life would even be possible.

And for my two boys, thank you for making me a momma, teaching me more about life, and giving me purpose. You are my greatest accomplishments. I hope my tales don't embarrass you too much.

table of contents

preface

I actually started writing this as an informational packet, not a book. After we were matched with our youngest son through CPS, people started seeing how cute he was, how well-adjusted and integrated into our family he was, and how "normal" an adoptive family could be. So several families we knew started to ask us about the process, as they may be interested in adoption as well.

Questions became more frequent, so I started putting together a little bit of information about our timeline and the ins and outs of the confusing and intricate foster care and adoption system. Those first drafts really did not have much about our story. But the deeper we went through the process and now finally being on the other side, I realized just how much support families waiting to be matched needed—a place to ask questions and express their fears, a community. So I started adding and adding to this "packet," and before I knew it, the packet looked more and more like a book, which brings us here.

I want to give you something that not only helps you feel confident about how adoption works, but makes you feel confident in saying "yes" to making adoption a reality for your family. While I talk in depth from our experience about the process and what to expect with adoption, I mostly want to share with you God's love and encourage you that He has a plan for our lives if we will only listen and be patient.

The first two sections of the book are about how we started to think about adoption for our family and our personal experiences throughout the process. The middle two sections are the meat and potatoes—what the requirements are, what the process leading up to adoption look likes, and how CPS and "the system" works once you have a child or children placed in your home. In the final section, I want to leave you with some tips on what to do while you are waiting and some additional resources that may be helpful and of interest to you throughout your adoption.

While our family adopted domestically through CPS and the foster-to-adopt program, this book is for any prospective adoptive parents, and 85 percent of the material will apply to anyone adopting, whether it be infant, domestic, or international adoption.

Part Four is the only section of the book devoted entirely to the inner workings of the CPS adoption process. While you can definitely gloss over this part if you are not adopting through CPS, I encourage you to still read it just to familiarize yourself with all aspects of adoption. Hey, you never know! I said I would never adopt through CPS myself.

While going through the adoption process myself, I found so many resources where adoptive parents shared how hard adoption is. Luckily, I knew God's call for my family and did not let those stories scare me off, but

I still felt really discouraged. So why the heck would I want to do that with this book?

I want to change the way I view and talk about adoption—and motherhood in general. It truly is an adventure. Sometimes during a camping trip (or in my case a glamping trip), you experience discomfort, setbacks, and frustrations—you trip and fall on a log; a raccoon eats all of your food while you are gone; you're hot, sweaty and tired. But those challenges do not minimize all the amazing experiences you have on your trip. Then, when you come home at the end of the trip, you look back and tell all the (now) funny stories that happened and hold tight to those amazing memories for years to come. I mean, look at the National Lampoon's Vacation movies. The franchise's five films have grossed over $300 million. Why are they so popular? Because we can all relate to these dream vacations. Add kids and road trips to the equation and who knows what chaos will ensue.

That is exactly what parenting and adoption is—a string of funny mishaps, wrong turns, and a lot of beautiful memories.

My hope in sharing my adoption adventure and my little family is that you will be encouraged to stay the course and that by the end, you feel like you got a big ol' hug, affirmation, and maybe even a few laughs at my shortcomings as a parent and housewife.

Every single family's story is different, but what we all have in common is the fear and anxiety of the unknown, and feeling alone in being a parent, especially in times your family and friends might not be able to relate to the path your family has chosen.

Throughout the book, I mention this several times (as it comes up in conversation every time I talk about adoption): I have never seen God's plan and love for me more than through the journey of motherhood and adoption. Of course it is always easier to see these things when reflecting on a completed chapter in your life. Just like reading stories from the Bible, it is so much easier to see God's lessons and provision in others stories than in our own life.

I love adoption, and I love sharing how God's faithfulness shines through it. I am literally praying for each and every one of you reading this—those of you who want to begin the adoption process, those of you who are right in the midst of being matched and those of you who are in the trenches of parenting, just like me. I hope you feel loved and encouraged.

xoxo

Holly Nicole James

PART *ONE*

The James Family Adventure - Our Story

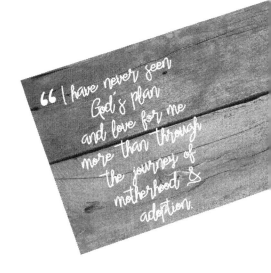

" I have never seen God's plan and love for me more than through the journey of motherhood & adoption.

Chapter 1:

Hello, My Name is Holly, and I am a "Gilmore Girls" Addict

Do you remember your first day of high school? I honestly do not. It wasn't much different than junior high for me. I had been to school with most of the same people since second grade. And since second grade, I had been the shy girl who sat at the front of the class, followed the rules, and tried to blend in the best that I could. But when you're 4'11" and 80 pounds, it's more difficult to blend in on your first day of high school than you might think. I was very okay not being the center of attention and quite frankly didn't care to "fit in."

I do, however, very much remember my first day of freshman camp in college. I was finally 5'4" and not 80 pounds anymore. I did not know anyone at school, and I had only met my roommate once at a freshman preview weekend. We hit it off and figured it would be better to room with someone we liked for a weekend than risk matching with a total stranger. But I did not really know anyone.

It hit me that no one else, at least the freshmen, really knew anyone either. They were probably just as nervous as I was, so why should I be shy? I decided the shy, quiet girl was the old, high school me and new, college me was not going to be timid or reserved. I had chosen to attend a small private university in Houston with only about 2,200 students (fewer than my high school), so that I could really get to know people.

Being a small school, college gave me the opportunity to do some pretty fun things—one of them being a freshman camping trip right before school started. We were split into various groups, stayed two or three nights away at a camp where upperclassmen acted as counselors, and had the chance to meet and mingle with our new fellow classmates. This was not my typical scene, but like I said, this was my chance to be the new, college me.

A fun fact about said camp is that they made every freshman wear a bright orange and royal blue, school-color beanie. And let me tell you, they were not cute. We were supposed to wear them for the duration of the camp and our first week of college. For the record, I complied for camp and camp only. Sporting a bright orange and blue beanie on my first day of college? Um yeah, no.

So wearing my hideous freshman beanie with my bags all packed, my roommate, other suitemates, and I all headed to the cafeteria to eat with all the other campers.

I grabbed a tray, went through the line, filled up my plate with food, utensils, and a drink, and headed to sit down. I located a table that I thought I might fit in at, put my tray down, and began to sit in my chair. What I did not realize, however, was that the corner of my tray was hanging slightly over the edge of the table. So as I went to sit down, my elbow caught the edge of the tray hanging off of the table, catapulting all the contents of my tray into the air and onto the floor.

Food and drink everywhere. And all eyes on yours truly. The only thing I could think to say was, "Hi, my name is Holly, and I am not very coordinated."

And that pretty much sums me up to this day.

So, hi, my name is Holly James, and I am not very coordinated. I am a 30-year-old working mom of two. I have been married to my best friend Jeremy for more than nine years, and we have been together since attending college at Houston Baptist University. Our oldest son, Clyde, is six-years-old and in first grade. He loves science, robotics, going to Awanas, and playing with the boys on our street. Our youngest son (for now), Nathaniel, just turned three and basically follows his older brother around everywhere. He likes Daniel Tiger, playing the ukulele, and exploring outside. Clyde came into the family through my pregnancy, and Nathaniel came into the family through local adoption with CPS.

I love fashion, but I don't love shopping for hours on end—mostly online shopping. I must have one large cup of coffee, which probably equates to more like two cups, in the morning. But I only press the button on the Keurig once, so I just count it as one. But perhaps the most important thing you need to know about me is that I am slightly obsessed with "Gilmore Girls". I currently own four "Gilmore Girls" t-shirts, I have

Luke's Diner mugs in my coffee bar, and I have watched the series in its entirety no less than a dozen times. I have been told I talk as fast as they do, and I secretly wish I was Lorelai Gilmore. And yes, since the revival Netflix show has come out, I have re-watched the original series (again), and I may or may not have watched the revival several times.

I digress.

Professionally, I specialize in marketing and design. I used to travel about a week a month for work, but now I travel more like once a quarter. I love what I do for a living. I am not wildly artistic like my soul yearns to be. I wish I could paint, draw, be a makeup/hair artist, master cake decorator—the whole nine yards. But I am pretty good at marketing, messaging and business analysis. And now I get to do that for my family's company instead of a corporation.

But my true passion and love—the one that keeps me up at night thinking about what the future holds—is my family and spreading God's love.

As I mentioned in the foreword, I started the process of writing this book because after we were matched with our youngest son, Nathaniel, a lot of families asked us about our adoption experience. I started creating a PDF pamphlet, which turned into a magazine that morphed into this book!

My hope for you is that through hearing about our adoption experience, your heart will be encouraged and open to whatever God has next for your family. We went through many ups and downs, a very long, sometimes challenging process, but we eventually were matched with our son, the sweet and spunky boy who God had planned to be a part of our family all along. We learned a lot along the way—mostly that the process is always different and God writes everyone's story differently—but through the process, we grew closer as a family, closer to God, and closer with our groups of friends.

First, I want to address a few misconceptions and fears about adoption. While I am sure some of these fears could manifest from hearing instances that these things have really happened, or from horror stories, I think a lot of times they are the minority. But if God is calling you to adopt, he will provide everything you need. I truly believe that.

1.) **Adoption is too expensive**. Yes, it can be! International adoption is very expensive. But there are a lot of grants you can apply for and fundraising opportunities you can take a part in. Infant adoption, when a birth mom chooses your family to adopt her child, can also be very costly. But again, grants and fundraising are helpful. However, there is a third adoption option. Through CPS, you can adopt local children in foster care who are waiting for a family. This type of adoption will just cost you lawyer fees to finalize the adoption. Depending on their policies, your adoption agency may even reimburse you for those costs. Realistically, you could pay $0 to $1,500 to adopt locally.

2.) **There are too many cultural issues to have a blended family**. There are (and will always be) people in this world who do not accept what they do not understand. Always. But for our blended family, these people have been a minority amongst our community and circle. We have also been blessed that our family and friends have not only accepted and embraced our black son, but they have loved him as equally as our oldest, biological son, with no distinction. This experience has shown us God in such a tangible way, and it has also given us an amazing—and obvious—way to witness to so many people around us.

Strangers actually stop us while we are on vacation, shopping, at the movies, eating, etc., to ask us our story. You see, we are young-ish, middle class white parents, with one white son and one black son, so it is pretty obvious that we have added to our family through adoption. Some people thank us. Some people offer their advice on how to care for our black son's hair. Some people want to know what in the world made us decide to something so unconventional. And yes, a lot of people want to know Nathaniel's story, how he came to be in the foster care system. While these interactions and conversations can range from being embarrassing, sweet, ill-timed, and sometimes even annoying, God showed us this was His biggest and easiest way for us to share the gospel of Jesus Christ to so many strangers.

3.) **Adoption may negatively affect my other children in the home**. This is how I look at it: If you were to get pregnant tomorrow, no one would look at you and say, "Why would you do that? You know your oldest son will be so messed up from the experience." I wanted to tell so many people that when we were in the paperwork stage of our adoption. You absolutely should consider your existing children in the home (age, stage of life, etc.), but as a parent, you already do that, no matter how you choose to grow your family. Yes, adoption is not necessarily mainstream, and you need to prepare your children for what is happening. And they will have questions. So many questions. But these conversations also help to form bonds with your children and teach them about God's unconditional love.

I heard this statistic Jayne Schooler read from her book during a session at a Created for Care mini retreat for foster, foster-to-adopt, and adoptive mommas: The majority of biological children who have adopted siblings tend to choose humanitarian professions, they are less judgmental of others, they have a greater acceptance of differences, and they manage crisis well.[1] That's amazing! So not only are we teaching them about God's unconditional love and having these big conversations early on, as foster and adoptive parents, we are also teaching our children to love so compassionately that they want to change the world.

If you had told me three years ago that I would be writing a book encouraging families to adopt, I honestly would have pointed and laughed at you. So before you read this book and think, "Great, another book from another perfect mom who has it all together telling me, 'You can do it, too,'" don't. You are in luck; I am none of those things. As I said, I am a working momma. I am not your perfect stay-at-home, Betty Crocker, have-it-all-together supermom (more on that later). I run late. I can't keep my house clean half of the time. I forget lunches on the counter. I love to wear sky-high heels. I am not your "traditional" mom. But I have a lot of love and a lot of fun to give. And I believe that's all that counts to be a good mom.

I only speak from my experience, and I know there are so many unique situations out there. I encourage you to speak to as many different

---

1 *Wounded Children, Healing Homes: How Traumatized Children Impact Adoptive and Foster Parents* by Jayne Schooler

sources as possible, to get a feel for what the adoption experience is really like. Talk to professionals in the field. Talk to other foster and adoptive families.

We had a lot of fears going into this chapter of our lives. And with any family, we've been through ups and downs, valleys and mountaintops. Being a parent is the hardest job in the world. But you can't let fears, uncertainties, and challenges stop you from doing what God is calling your family to do. You could miss out on the biggest blessing and greatest journey in each one of your family member's lives.

Chapter 1:
Unplanned Adoption

The title of this chapter is funny to me because it starts with "unplanned." Unplanned is not a word I usually use or like to use. In fact, it usually has a negative connotation, right? Unplanned expenses. Unplanned surgery. Unplanned maintenance. All things we try to avoid.

Ask my friends who try to make a dinner date with me. I have to check my calendar and plan weeks in advance. Between kid schedules, doctor appointments, work, church/church events, and birthday parties, my schedule tends to fill up quickly. I'm just like Jane from "27 Dresses" and her massive planner with notes everywhere. I like to plan for things to ensure my life runs as smoothly as possible.

And even though I may know that a birthday party is coming weeks in advance, I still purchase the gift the day of the party every. single. time. But hey, at least I am consistent.

So to have a huge, unplanned life event, is really uncharacteristic of me.

Our decision to adopt was not made immediately, and it wasn't something we had planned at this stage in our life. At the young age of 11, I decided God called me to adopt a girl from China because of their laws on population control. I carried this calling with me for years, and it was actually one of my "must-accept" boxes, which Jeremy gladly agreed to, when looking for a spouse. This was a when-I-am-older-and-established ideal, but God had placed that love in my heart for the rest of our story to grow.

We had Clyde, our biological son, in 2010 when I was 23 and Jeremy was 27. We had been married for a short time and were struggling to establish our careers and family life. Fast forward two years, and we felt more grounded in our marriage and financials so we started talking about when would be the right time to have a second child.

I really did not enjoy pregnancy. I didn't have a lot of medical problems, but picture my very tiny body with a very big Clyde working full-time in the middle of a hot Texas summer. It just was not my favorite experience, which I will forever feel guilty about, but the result, our sweet baby boy, was so wanted and loved, of course. All this to say, my experience made my decision to be pregnant again a hard one to make.

One day, Jeremy said, "So, I had this really weird dream I wanted to talk to you about. I had this dream that we adopted a little black boy domestically. What do you think?"

Side note: As the planners we are, we do not typically base our major family decisions on dreams. And I usually think people are weird who tell these types of stories! Well, I am now apparently one of those "weird" people who make life decisions based on dreams and think God communicated with us that way. Please welcome me to the club.

I also had never considered domestic adoption as an option for expanding our family and definitely did not consider adopting multiple children making myself an "adoption mom"—you know like Angelina Jolie. I am so not that cool at all.

So we began to pray about it.

Expanding Our Family Through Adoption

After thinking and praying quite a bit, we finally decided domestic adoption would be the path for our family, and we would apply for the Domestic, African-American Infant program, a very specific program offered by a Christian agency recommended by my former boss. We applied to their program in January 2013 and shortly after received the crushing letter that they were not accepting any more parents into their program at that time due to lack of birth mothers.

After mourning this for a few months, we heard that CPS in Houston was hosting an information meeting about foster care, foster-to-adopt, and adoption. I never had a desire to adopt through CPS and definitely never wanted to foster, but we decided to attend just to hear what they had to say. And hey, maybe they had some infant programs we were unaware of.

The meeting was full, a room of about 100 people. A veteran CPS worker and supervisor gave a beautiful presentation covering statistics of kids in foster care, stories of some of the children, and the mechanics of the process.

> The first time our hearts *broke* was when we found out sibling sets and minority children have been classified as *special needs* by CPS.

The first time our hearts broke during the presentation was when we found out that sibling sets and minority children over the age of two have been classified in a "special needs" category because their adoptive placements are so hard to find. They even added benefits, such as free college to any state school, to these programs to give parents an incentive to adopt this group.

Then, we heard a story that still sticks out in my mind to this day. CPS was having a hard time placing an older child in a home that would be a good match. The child had been moved to several homes, and his current home was effectively considered his last chance. Around 2 a.m. one night, the CPS supervisor received a phone call from the boy's foster parents saying he was not allowed to live with them anymore, and CPS needed to come get this boy right away. The supervisor tried calming the foster parents down but they said no, they would not change their minds and the boy was already waiting for him on the porch with a trash bag of his things.

> And if I may interrupt myself for a minute, this trash bag scenario is sadly not uncommon. Many kids in foster care have very few possessions, including luggage or a duffel bag, and many times they are removed from their homes with their belongings in trash bags. This is a very real and all too often occurrence.

Anyway, back to the story. When the CPS supervisor arrived at the foster home, he went straight to the boy to ask details of what happened. He found out the teenager had thrown a brick through an upstairs window, shattering it. The incident was the last straw for his foster parents. When the supervisor asked the boy why he did this, which was of no concern to the foster parents at this point, he replied that it was his birthday, and no one had even remembered. His intention wasn't necessarily to cause trouble. His outburst was simply a reaction to sadness and frustration. I mean, how would you feel if someone forgot your birthday?

No doubt one of many similar stories. But after I heard this, my heart softened, and I realized that maybe, just maybe, kids in CPS care were not "unfixable" like the stereotypes and stigmas told me. Maybe they were just kids who had experienced a lot of bad, hard circumstances that were weighing them down without anyone ever asking about their lives.

Our hearts broke wide open when Q&A time began to close out this beautiful and eloquent presentation. As quickly as the presenter asked if anyone had questions, the first two questions were "How much do we get paid monthly to be foster parents?" and "Do you pay for their clothes?" Immediately following the answers, 75 percent of the room of 80 to 100 people cleared and only a handful of couples were left who wanted to adopt.

Yes, this really happened.

We decided then and there that domestic adoption through CPS was the right call for our family.

After that meeting, we attended a "Wait No More" Conference put on by a partnership of the State of Texas and churches to get more families involved in the adoption process. The great part about this conference was that all the adoption agencies in the greater Houston area attended, and we were able to gather information, speak to their representatives, and take all this home with us to review and pick an adoption agency. This is a HUGE decision! (See chapter 7 on why we chose our agency and things to look for.)

We chose to work with our agency for many reasons, the most important being that they are a Christian organization and do work for communities all around the world. We began the adoption process wanting to go the route of Waiting Texas Children, looking to adopt children whose biological parents already terminated their rights, leaving them legally available for adoption. But since we wanted to adopt a child two-years-old and under (to keep Clyde's birth order), we realized that the quickest and best path for us would be to pursue foster-to-adopt with legal risk placements.

/verb/ **fos•ter-to-a•dopt**

fōstər tōō ə ´däpt

Foster-to-adopt places the child in a home that intends to adopt the child in which birth parents' rights have not yet been severed by the court or in which birth parents are appealing the court's decision but foster parents agree to adopt the child if/when parental rights are terminated. Social workers place the child with specially-trained foster-to-adopt parents who will work with the child during family reunification efforts but who will adopt the child if the child becomes available for adoption. The main reason for making such a placement is to spare the child another move.[2]

/verb/ le•gal risk place•ment

legal risk plasment

Legal risk placement is when a child is placed with a prospective adoptive family, and the child is not yet legally free for adoption. A child becomes legally free once a parent's parental rights are terminated or the parents have relinquished their parental rights. In the case of a legal risk placement, either the termination hasn't occurred yet or it has and is being contested in court by the birth family. When a family takes in a child who is considered to be a legal risk placement that family must understand that the child may be placed back with his birth family. This is not just a legal risk in terms of the courts, but a risk of the prospective adoptive family's hearts.[3]

---

2 https://adoption.com/wiki/Foster-Adoption_(Glossary)

3 https://adoption.com/wiki/Legal_Risk_Adoptions

The decision to pursue legal risk placements was hard for us because not only do Jeremy and myself run the risk of forming an attachment with a child who could be removed from our home, Clyde had that risk as well, and we didn't know if we wanted to put him through that.

However, we were told most children who are considered legal risk have been moved from CPS' goal of reunification with the birth family to adoption placement outside of relatives, making the risk well, less risky. We were also told that legally-free children ages two and under are the most sought after, not to mention we limited it to males only, and that this could make our process go longer if we choose not to include legal risk children.

So we began the paperwork process and started moving quickly with our required classes, preparing for a new child to enter our family.

While we didn't plan our family to be an "adoptive family," it surely doesn't minimize the impact adoption has had on our lives. I still can't really believe that the whole topic of domestic adoption even came up because of a dream that Jeremy had. The best laid plans, huh? I'm grateful that God's plan for me is so much better than what I could even imagine, because I certainly would not have imagined this life at all.

Chapter 3:
Our Support System

I grew up with a small immediate family but a large extended family—and most of us lived within 10 minutes of each other. My parents were both one of five children. The family actually all got along for the most part and loved hanging out with each other.

We had dinner at my paternal grandmother's house every weeknight, celebrated birthdays together, and did an annual progressive dinner with different courses of the meal at different houses. Every year, we had a Styron Family Shrimp Boil with traditional picnic games like egg toss and sack races. We also loved playing pranks on each other, like leaving a can of decorated pickled pigs feet on each other's door step (don't ask, maybe it's a southern/Texas thing?) and making life-sized ornaments to declare who was Mawmaw's "favorite" grandchild.

My mom's parents also lived 10 minutes away. My Cajun Mawmaw was a teacher with a private Montessori pre-school and kindergarten in her house, which I attended when I was young. We picked my Mawmaw and Pawpaw up every Saturday to go shopping, and she made her coveted gumbo with a roux renowned chefs envied. When I was younger, my mom worked for Continental Airlines (I'm showing my age as they were bought out by United and no longer exist), and we traveled the world on standby with them after they had both retired.

We all still get together for birthdays, holidays, annual shrimp boils, and progressive dinners—traditions I truly, truly treasure and feel grateful to be able to pass to my boys. We even talk to my parents, sister, and niece every day on FaceTime and see them in person at least once a week.

This close connection with my large family instilled in me at a young age a deep sense of comfort, belonging, self-assurance, and wisdom. So going through grade school without a lot of friends was no big deal. My best friends were my family. Not to mention we had wonderful family and church friends. We had a great solid base and community.

So as I started growing my family, these values were very important to me to establish with my children. I knew the importance of family and close friends who stepped in as family.

But there was a key piece missing from our circle when we chose to make adoption a reality for our family. We didn't know anyone who had adopted or was going through the adoption process. We were the first. And even though we knew of a few families who had adopted, they had mostly gone through international adoption. No one, I mean no one, we had ever met had adopted through CPS. So we were quite a shock and original in our circle, setting out on uncharted territory.

However, in the midst of choosing to adopt, Jeremy had been hired to a new position at our church, The Bridge Fellowship in Sugar Land, which we had attended since college. We were opening a new portable campus in the Palladium Theater, and they needed a media director, which matched Jeremy's skill set perfectly. We needed this in our marriage so badly, and we had no idea at the time how this would be the best thing that could ever happen to our family.

At the time, he was working Tuesdays, Thursdays, and Sundays. This allowed him to spend quality time with our then 2.5-year-old (and fast forward a few years and add an 8-month-old). This gave us the flexibility we needed to meet with our social workers and make all the appointments we needed.

But the biggest blessing that came from the position is that once we started becoming actively involved at this new campus, we met several families who had adopted children or were in the process of adopting—international, domestic, infant, foster, you name it. We had a solid support system to lean on even though all of our stories and experiences are very different. Just having someone understand, even in the smallest capacity during this process, was huge in us making it through.

The friends I made during this time are still some of my dearest friends I have today. We have been through so much together. We have prayed through the waiting time, the matching process, legal battles, temper tantrums, medical diagnoses, adjusting periods, sibling rivalry, money and marriage issues, and sickness. And we have celebrated matches, milestones, adoption finalizations, overcoming physical and mental challenges, birthdays, making new friends, and becoming so much a part of a community.

There are times that emotionally, my adoptive mommas get me on a different level. I liken these people to war friends, having weathered storms and challenges only they can relate to and understand. I felt a loss so deep for each child we applied for that we were not matched with. In some ways, I felt each time like I actually lost a child. Many of our friends and family would sympathize but thought I was being a little overly emotional. No, it was not miscarriage or death, but my adoptive mommas knew intimately that feeling of loss, even if their experience had been slightly different.

Especially once we were matched, I found that there are some things an adoptive mom and child must do differently than with a biological child. Sometimes, people think your child's behaviors and challenges are just "normal kid things," but as an adoptive mom, you know they are a result of past trauma in a child's life, and they need extra time, attention, and love. My adoptive mommas knew that and could advise me from that perspective and common experience.

The moment I realized just how important these adoptive momma friends really are is when a sweet friend organized a mini Created for Care weekend retreat.

The original Created for Care event is a conference and retreat designed specifically for women in the throes of foster care and/or adoption. It is a nonprofit ministry designed to equip parents with encouragement and adoption resources for the upcoming year. This retreat only offers 500 spots and fills up within minutes of tickets being available. It has become so popular that at first they added a second weekend for more moms to be able to attend. They have since created a schedule, curriculum, and video sessions for people to use to create local, mini replicas of this event.

My friend had attended the large gathering every year and always came home with a sense of direction for her family and what God wanted for her for the upcoming year. So she wanted to bless her fellow adoptive friends with a similar retreat. She did not know how many would or could attend, but she reached out to myself and my two other adoptive momma friends at church to ask what dates would work for us so that she could plan the weekend around our schedules. Her event had 25 spots that filled up immediately.

Let me just interject with a little bit of backstory. I do not like sleepovers. I never have. Even in high school I was like Cinderella—the clock struck midnight, and I was ready to be back in my own bed. I used to think I just was not a "girl person." I didn't need a lot of girlfriends in my life because I did not need drama, and I am not a share-my-feelings, wear-matching-t-shirts, swap-make-up-tips kind of gal. I get my makeup at Walgreens for goodness' sake.

So as amazing as this invitation was and as much as I wanted to go and get away on a beautiful retreat, it was also a little bit outside of my comfort zone. Not to mention I was going to have to drive myself a couple of hours to the location after work on a Friday. I had to figure out what to do with the boys because Jeremy had to work on Sundays, starting at 4 a.m. And Nathaniel was still under CPS care, so he couldn't spend the night anywhere else. So it just made things complicated. Remember that crazy planner book I told you about? Now you may understand a little better why I need one! So I decided to split the difference. I would stay one night and come back early on Saturday before dark to take over the boys. Knowing me, I would probably would be ready to come home anyway.

Never have I been more wrong.

I didn't want to leave at all. Not one little bit. It was the perfect mix of socializing, hearing stories from other mommas in all spectrums of adoption—those wanting to adopt, who have adopted, had multiple adoptions, infant adoptions, international adoptions, foster care, older adoptions, sibling sets, special needs, all of the above. We ended up having 22 adoptive/foster mommas with a whopping 84 kids among us. 49 of those children joined our families via adoption or fostering, five more children were waiting to come home, and eight different countries were represented. So when I say all spectrums of adoption, I do believe we had it covered for this "mini" session.

There was worship music, break out sessions, prayer time, and just the simplicity of sharing a meal with friends without a kid sitting in your lap and eating off of your plate or asking you to take them to the bathroom right when you sit down.

I had no idea how badly my soul needed rest, needed to connect with other mommas who had been there. Or been through something better. Or worse. Or someone to genuinely say, "I get your fears, and I want to pray for you."

This is why I say you need at least one adoptive momma you can turn to who encourages you to go to retreats you didn't even know you needed to attend. I encourage you to find a person or a group now to lean on. Your agency may be a good resource for this or even try to find online adoption groups through social media. But I really feel this was crucial for us. Having someone who has been through it to encourage you, give advice from a different perspective, and swap stories is just what we needed.

Our family and friends are the greatest and most loving support system we could ever have. Just how the Trinity works, three in one, so does our support system, which is made up of a mix of fellow adoptive families, childhood friends I cherish dearly, and family. Without them we could not have made it through anything we did and continue to do. This is absolutely not the time to shut out your friends and family members just because they may not understand all of the ins and outs of adoption.

My parents were there to watch Clyde on the weekends when we had to drive an hour and a half to our adoption agency, only then to stay for eight hours of classes, and then drive an hour and a half home. We had sweet friends and family members shower us with a party to welcome our newest little addition and officially welcome him into our circle. And my dear, dear friends love my boys as much as I do and celebrate their accomplishments, pray for them when they are sick, and encourage them in their faith.

You need every person you can in your corner helping you and your children. You need a tribe made up of all of these people—adoptive friends, family members, and friends who are just like family. (Note: This essential community is not to be confused with a squad like Taylor Swift. Those coveted positions rotate as much as I change my outfits.)

You need emotional and physical support. You need people to encourage you, watch your kids, and bring you dinner.

Even if you don't have all the pieces to your support system set up in your life right now, I am sending a big hug, lots of coffee, and so much encouragement and understanding.

1 Cor 10:13

"But God is *faithful*; He will not suffer you to be tempted beyond that which you are able to bear, but with the temptation will also make a way to *escape*, that you may be able to bear."

God loves you, sweet friend. And He has not given you more than you can handle. You are His daughter or His son, and He wants the very best for you—even if it is hard to see from where you are standing. This calling God has put on your family, will stretch you, try you, and make you lean on Him every step of the way. In that time, you will know love more fiercely, and I really believe you will be brought closer to God than you ever knew was possible. I didn't even know what support I needed, and God moved our careers and our lives to a place where these friendships and this community was possible. So, I know He can do that for you, too.

Chapter 4:

Our Adoption Timeline

Good things come to those who wait.

Patience is a virtue.

Everything in its time.

Everything happens for a reason.

We have all heard these clichés about waiting. Heck, we may have even used these to teach our kids a lesson, even though we swore we wouldn't. But seriously, how helpful are these when we are truly waiting for something for which our heart longs, something that we wait years for?

Going into it, I knew that this adoption thing was not a quick process, but wow! It is not a quick process. I mean if you think about the significance of matching a child, their wants, needs, dispositions, medical history, and personality, with a family that has wants, needs, dispositions, medical histories, and personalities, you can begin to realize why it takes so long.

People have different expectations of the time this process will take. People especially love to publish the "Oh my gosh! We started this process and got matched three months later" stories. But I wanted to share with you our timeline so you can get an idea of how long things can take and also gives you a look into the process and order of how things progress.

James Family Adoption Timeline

Started Adoption Process
January 2013
Applied to Infant Adoption Program. Rejected.

Accepted into Agency
May 2013

Completed Classes
September 2013
Completed all requirements including classes, home study, CPR certification, background check, and fingerprinting

Licensed by State of Texas
February 2014
Same day Nate is born

RAS Meeting & Matched
September 2014

First Time to Meet Nate
October 10, 2014

Permanent Placement
October 24, 2014

Parental Rights Terminated
March 12, 2015

April 2015
Moved to adoption services with CPS and Adoption Agency

May 15, 2015
Applied for redacted file with CPS

August 25, 2015
Signed adoption placement papers & applied for adoption finalization court date

Adoption Finalized!
September 23, 2015

From start to finish, this was a 33-month process, just shy of three years. Now, this timeline also included us being rejected from a program and moving to another.

If you notice from the timeline, once we actually got started, it only took us about four months to blow through all of the paperwork and training requirements. This is what I like to refer to as the "honeymoon period." You're excited, determined, and optimistic. You feel like you are accomplishing things because you have a checklist, things to do, and goals to work toward. But once you finish that checklist, the rest is completely out of your hands. If you are even remotely Type A and take-charge like I am, that is the worst thing you can hear. Out. Of. Your. Hands.

We waited for about a year until we were matched. The bulk of our process was living in the waiting period. I cannot stress to you enough, and I will several times in several different places throughout the book, how important what you do in the waiting time is. Almost 40 percent of our process was waiting. Now, I know what you are thinking, "well that is just your experience."

And you are right. I am definitely not suggesting that our experience will be your exact timeline. Deep in the back of my mind, I know I felt like I was going to be the exception to the rule. That these timelines were accurate for most people, but somehow I was such an amazing person and mother that I definitely would be the exception.

Listen, I hope you are the exception. But what if you aren't? I really suggest preparing yourself as best as you can for this. I know a year doesn't seem long. But when you are in the middle of this waiting period, it feels much, much longer.

I think what made the waiting process feel even longer for me is the fact that so many people constantly asked questions about the status of our adoption process. Did we have any updates? Had we been matched? What did the timeline look like? Of course, they are just trying to be kind, express interest, and make conversation. Of course, they genuinely cared about us and desperately wanted us to be matched as much as we did. But to me, it felt like a little paper cut every time someone asked, knowing I had to say, "still nothing," trying to say it cheery without looking like my soul was secretly being crushed.

I also wanted to share this information with you because most of the scope of the timeline adoption agencies share online begins once you start the process with them and ends with being matched with a child. Most agencies will say this looks like a 12-to-24-month time period. And while this is not inaccurate, they do not typically explain how long it can take you to find an agency, and they definitely leave out the what's to come after placement. That totally changes the way the timeline looks.

And agencies do this for a reason! Pretty much every family who starts the process wants to know the time frame for having a child in their home. That is all us adoptive families care about. When do I get to meet my child? Of course these were my same thoughts and feelings as well, which is why I wanted to put the overall process in perspective for you and share what the timeline really looks like. You're not alone.

I recommend that you keep track of these dates for yourself. What ends up inevitably happening is that during the waiting process you begin to add the months of finding an adoption agency into your timeline. So, for example, in your mind you may have been waiting 12 months, but you only started working with the agency five months ago. This puts more pressure on your case manager and gives yourself unrealistic expectations for when the matching process could happen for you and your family.

So instead of giving you that same old cliché, "good things come to those who wait," I want to leave you with some truth that you can bury in your heart.

Have you ever studied some of the Jewish customs during biblical times? It sounds old and boring, but some of them were actually quite fascinating and detailed. Knowing these traditions helps make so many weird biblical references actually make sense. One of my favorites is the betrothal period, or what we would now called engagement period, during the Jewish wedding traditions.

Before a couple would even become betrothed, there was an arranged marriage process and even written marriage contracts and bridal payments. Before you get upset about that, the bridal payment went to the groom's family but was ultimately for the bride to set her "free" from her parent's household. Different times people, different times.

Anyway, after all of these transactions were complete, there was a one-year betrothal period. What is so interesting about this is that 1) the couple was apart, each preparing for the wedding, and 2) they were actually in a covenant, legal marriage during this time. So even if you wanted out at this point, you would have to file for a divorce, even though the wedding had not happened yet.

During this year, the groom is adding on additions to the house where he currently lives with his family to make room for him and his new bride and family to come. (I'm not even going to touch on the fact that they will be living with their in-laws the rest of their lives, as that is not the point. Another discussion for another time.) The bride-to-be uses this time to prepare her clothes and herself for the wedding day and prepare for being a wife.

But here is the most interesting part to me: She knew approximately when her husband-to-be would be coming back, but she did not know the exact day or time when he would be coming back. Yep, no cell phones back then to text and say, "Hey babe, I'm ready. Get your stuff together." Nope. She had to be ready to go at all times!

I think of this custom often when I think of adoption. We have a kind-of-sort-of-not-really idea of how the whole process works. We have an idea of the approximate timeline. But we have no idea when exactly that call is going to come. We have no idea when we are finally going to meet the son or daughter God has planned for us.

But we, too, have a "betrothal period" to wait and prepare for this child to come. So instead of using it wishing that day were here, I encourage you to use this time preparing yourself for what is to come. Find yourself some adoptive mommas. Go on dates with your spouse, especially if you do not already have children. Go on as many dates as possible! Because after kids, it's all, "Dates, what are dates?" That's when you miraculously don't have kids for the evening, and you're so exhausted that you place a to-go order from your favorite restaurant, rent a movie on Amazon, chat a little, and fall asleep by 10 p.m. right? And fill yourself with the Word and truth to become confident in God's wisdom and plan for your life.

I promise you will thank me later—when you don't even have time to finish your whole cup of coffee while it's still warm, and your quiet time is the two seconds you steal to go to the bathroom.

Notes

PART *TWO*
What I Wish I Would Have Known

" I promise you, God hears the cries of your heart and is taking care of you so much more than he takes care of the birds.

Chapter 5:
Letter to My Past Self

Sitting here, watching my two crazy boys run around, thinking about the profound effect of what God has done for our family. It's almost overwhelming at times, really. I still can't believe God chose me to be both of my kids' mom. And I can't believe how much we went through to get here.

We had no one to hold our hands through this. We had no one to look up to, no one to talk to who had ever gone through this process. We really and truly almost walked through this blind. (But, hey, that is how parenthood goes most of the time, right?) I was a young, 26-year-old, working and traveling momma with a 2-year-old, hoping to adopt another little boy. How that must have looked!

Now that I am a little older and a little wiser, I wish I could go back in time with the knowledge I have now. If I could mail a letter to my past self, a la "The Lake House," it would read something like this:

Dear young and somewhat naive 26-year-old Holly,

You are entering the most crucial, critical, and life-changing event of your life so far. Right now, you think that because you have a good home, a sweet little two-year-old, and a good support system, you are helping a little kid out there who needs a family. And while, yes you are, you have no idea that this little boy is about to turn your world upside down and will be the key to change your heart, soul, and purpose in life.

You are so hopeful and so eager. Don't ever lose sight of that. I know it is hard to wait, and I know the unknown is scary. I know there are people around you who do not completely understand why you feel the need to make such a "drastic" decision so young in life. Everyone around you, strangers included, will give you advice or the bug-eyed look of "Oh really? You are going to ADOPT?" They may even try to talk you out of doing what they think is weird or won't be accepted by others.

But is that really different than other times in your life you have done things that were "weird" or that people thought you were crazy for because you were answering God's call? Like not drinking when everyone else was. Or going to a Christian college that had less people than your high school and where boys weren't even allowed in the girls' dorm after the sun went down. Or getting married the month after you graduated college.

That's just the cost of following what God calls you to do sometimes. I guess that's why God left us so many stories in the Bible of people who loved Him and had to go through the same things. Well not the same thing, I mean Daniel was thrown in a den with actual lions. But God saved him, and He will walk you through this, as well.

And to be honest, you can bet that if there is so much opposition to what you are doing, you are probably right where God wants you. So stay the course. All those fears will keep you from doing what God is most definitely calling you to do. The people who do not understand what you are doing are just scared, but they will eventually see God's hand in every bit of this situation.

There will be times in the process that you will not understand why you must wait. Your little heart will cry out from sadness and the desire to hold your son who is out there somewhere. But please believe me when I tell you, God is making you wait, not to test your patience, but because He is lining up everything for your son to be brought to you. And those things take time! I promise, the first time you meet your son all of these challenges will be so absolutely worth it, and you will begin to understand this whole process.

The worst thing about waiting is the quiet. And you have time to think. You will think about every possible scenario—what could happen, what should happen, what ifs, doubts and fears of getting older, and your family not being mapped out just like you planned.

Adoption is not like pregnancy where you know the approximate due date/end time. Remember how Clyde was a week late in the hottest part of the summer, and you were oh so mad that he refused to make his debut? Yeah, take that week of waiting, multiply that by months, and add in the fear of the unknown.

Matthew 6:26-27

"Look at the **birds of the air**;
they do not sow or reap or
store away in the barns, and
yet your heavenly Father feeds
you. Are you not much more
valuable than they? Can any
one of you add by worrying
add a single hour to your life?"

But don't forget what God said in Matthew 6:26-27, "Look at the birds of the air; they do not sow or reap or store away in the barns, and yet your heavenly Father feeds you. Are you not much more valuable than they? Can any one of you add by worrying a single hour to your life?"

Every time you are sad, try to lean into your sweet little family. You won't get this time back when it's only the three of you. Cherish each and every moment because your life will change in so many ways. And I promise you, God hears your cries and is taking care of you so much more than He does of the birds.

While you wait, you will then have to do the hardest thing you have ever had to do. You will have to look through the profiles of so many children—reading about their lives, their needs, their little souls—and you will have to make the grueling decision of whether a child would potentially be a good fit for you and your family or not.

Lean into the Lord during this time. Bury His Word, His truth, and His promises. He is good and has the best thing planned for you and is using this time to change your heart. You have no idea there are so many children in a 40-mile radius who have experienced so much trauma, abuse, and chaos in their short, little lives. Use that information to change how you view the world, and let the compassion, love, and generosity in your heart grow.

People are going to ask you questions. A lot of questions. SO many questions. Some are out of curiosity. Some are out of love. And some are, unfortunately, out of utter and complete ignorance. You will no doubt get frustrated and want to feel like a "normal" parent. Well, guess what. You are not a normal parent. And that is amazing. You are teaching your children to see the world from a different perspective. You are teaching them to love fiercely and without borders.

And you are also teaching those lessons to those around you. You really have no idea right now the kind of impact your family will have on them. So many hearts will change how they view adoption, how they view children in CPS, and yes, even how they see people of other races and a mixed family. So respond with dignity and grace, and know that your children are looking up to you to see how you respond.

Try coming up with canned answers so that you won't be thrown off guard. You will be asked a lot of questions, especially at first, that run the gamut of: "Why in the world would you want to adopt?" "Do you have fertility issues?" "What is your son's story—why was he in CPS care in the first place?" and "Do you get looked at funny for being a mixed family?"

Let people know the real reason why you decided to adopt. Let them know it's because God put a love for children without a home in your heart at a very young age. And that you realized you have an amazing home, support system, and a whole lot of love to give that some child was just waiting for you to give them, and that it was the best thing you ever did for yourself and for your family.

Most importantly, know that you don't have to answer every single question asked of you. You do not owe everyone the whole story. Even though you love pleasing people, and you love sharing, some things are meant just for you to keep in your heart.

I know you think this is all difficult right now. But you have no idea. The most difficult part is not the process, it's not dealing with CPS, and it's not managing medical issues. The most difficult part of this whole experience is handling the ins and outs of being a mom every day. You *will wonder if issues you are dealing with are due to adoption, trauma, or it they are just normal kid things. You will worry if you are putting your family in the best situations that account for the diversity both of the boys need. You will worry if you work too much, if you are involved enough, and if you give each child 50/50 attention.*

My best advice to you is to stop being so critical of yourself. God set you on this path. He placed these babies in your care because He knew what was best for you and them. You have a deep-seated strength and perseverance that God has gifted you with that you have no idea you even possess. But you have a momma bear spirit, ready to go to bat and protect your children no matter what.

Enjoy this time with your babies because you can never get it back. The way to be the best mom is to just be present and active. Because even if you get a few of the little things wrong, you are giving your all. You are cultivating their talents and interests, and you are showing them God's love and teaching them to love the Lord. That's the best gift you can give them and yourself.

Psalm 127:3-5: "Children are a heritage from the Lord, offspring a reward from him. Like arrows in the hands of a warrior are children born in one's youth. Blessed is the man whose quiver is full of them. They will not be put to shame when they contend with their opponents in court."

The legacy you leave behind is NOT the quality of your Instagram feed. It's not about how cute you are, how perfectly decorated your house is, or how well dressed your children are. Let your legacy be that you loved other people more than yourself. Raise your family as arrows for the Lord. And let your decision to adopt put your priorities in crystal clear focus.

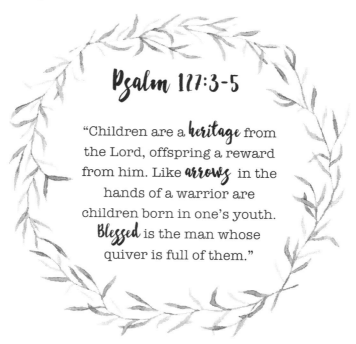

Psalm 127:3-5

"Children are a *heritage* from the Lord, offspring a reward from him. Like *arrows* in the hands of a warrior are children born in one's youth. *Blessed* is the man whose quiver is full of them."

Keep the course, and keep giving your heart and your love. With those as your goals, you can never go wrong.

xoxo

Your future self x

Chapter 6:

I'm Not a Martha Stewart Mom, and You Don't Have to be Either!

Do you remember in school how the big assignment you had to complete, almost every year, was "What I Want to Do and Be When I Grow Up." My life as a wife and mom are not the vision I had for myself. I certainly never wrote about that in my essay.

My original plan was to be this 30-something, independent career women, traveling and taking over the world, perfectly poised in a boardroom. I don't know what I envisioned myself doing in the boardroom, but I knew I would look fabulous doing it with a huge cup of Starbucks in my hand.

Then, I was married at 21, and I was pregnant with my oldest son at 22. I had been married about a-year-and-a-half when Clyde came along. So scratch that jet-setting, corporate mom dream. I then changed the ideal vision of myself as a have-it-all-together wife and mother—a June Cleaver—type all decked out in Ann Taylor. Ha. Don't get me wrong, I still love me some Ann Taylor on occasion, but I am definitely not that conventional person every day. I like weird, runway fashion, Harajuku girls, fringe, sparkles, and my life mantra is, "The higher the heel the closer to God."

My two visions for myself were just totally contradictory. What I forgot to factor in was that I still have a passion for marketing, and I love working. I am not very conventional in how I dress, I don't like doing housework for hours on end, and I don't like to attend PTA meetings. That said, I still really like my kids and husband, and I would rather spend time with them than hang out at some trendy bar in midtown on a random Tuesday night.

In fact, just to prove to you how much of a non-soccer mom I truly am, let me tell you about the first room mom meeting I attended when Clyde started kindergarten at a local private school. It was absolutely comical. The room was full of 30-something, stay-at-home moms in their perfect athletic wear with Smart Water and/or homemade juice puree. And in comes this 20-something working mom (that's me), sporting skinny jeans with a hole in the knee, a venti Starbucks, a blazer, and black heels (that I fell in love with because they looked like a pair from "Sons of Anarchy"). Yep, I totally fit in. Thank goodness for a sweet mom I met there who had already been a room mom. She took pity on me and helped me through the year of rigorous demands. Without her, I would have been eaten alive.

Side note: If you do resemble this vision of the have-it-all-together, Martha Stewart mom, I am so jealous of you. This blonde girl with fake eyelashes will be first in line to buy your book about how to be more like you. But regardless if you are either types of these women, or a different one altogether, you are still in good company!

In all seriousness, I think that the biggest misconception about adoption is that you need to be the essence of all moms to mother a child someone else birthed. In some ways, we seem to think that if you are going to be an adoptive mom (said in a royal, fancy British voice), you must be a better mom, right? You must be this overly compassionate, caring, patient, loving person. You must love all children and all people. You probably even regularly go to disease-ridden, third world countries to help cure everyone and fix every problem.

I can't tell you how many times people have approached us to thank us for "what we do." What we do? Did I just put the grocery cart up with all the other carts instead of leaving it in the aisle? Did I just keep my kids contained as not to bother anyone around us? Oh, you meant thank you for adopting. I guess I am just unconformable getting thanked because I feel like it insinuates that I am supposed to be the amazing mom I mentioned above. Little do you know, I'm so "amazing" that I successfully put on clothes and makeup (a rare combo) on while getting both kids dressed - with matching socks on top of that. I am totally rocking this mom thing!

I think God's greatest lesson that He is always teaching us, myself included, is that this life we live here on Earth, IS NOT ABOUT US. It has always been, and will always be, about God and His glory.

I think of when God was telling Moses His plan for him, that he,

Moses, was going to lead the Israelites out of captivity from the Egyptians. I picture myself in Moses' shoes and would absolutely be like, "Yeah, um, Lord, that's great and all, but um, no. I don't think so. I am shy and timid and well…not a leader."

Moses actually did say that to the Lord in Exodus 4:10, "Please, Lord, I have never been eloquent, neither recently nor in time past, nor since You have spoken to Your servant; for I am slow of speech and slow of tongue." He legitimately had a stutter.

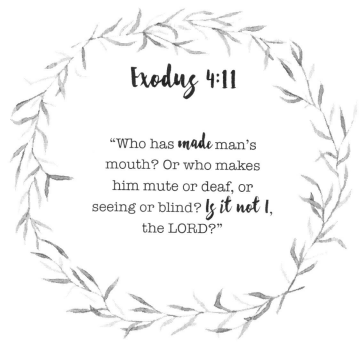

Exodus 4:11

"Who has **made** man's mouth? Or who makes him mute or deaf, or seeing or blind? **Is it not I**, the LORD?"

And then God responds to Him in such a beautiful and unexpected way in verse 11: "Who has made man's mouth? Or who makes him mute or deaf, or seeing or blind? Is it not I, the LORD?" God basically tells Moses,

"Did I not make you? Don't you think I know you have a stutter? If I made that in you, do you think I can't take it from you?"

This is true for you, too, beautiful momma. You are not perfect, and I am not perfect. Even if you do have the perfect outfit for the occasion. Life does not always turn out the way we planned or how we envisioned it. The faster you meditate on this and let that truth live in your heart, the faster you can learn to lean on God to be what you cannot be.

Being Martha Stewart is not what makes you a good mom. Not even a little. And let's be honest—the real Martha Stewart isn't even "Martha Stewart" all the time! She has made some mistakes herself. But the way you love and raise your children is what should define you as a momma.

There have been many days I have told my husband, "Man, I was just not a good mom today." And do you want to know his response? "No, you had one bad day. That does not make you a bad mom."

What makes you a good parent is you showing up, full of love, all day, every day. That is it. That is why I wanted to adopt in the first place, and maybe it is your motivation, too. I had so much love in my heart that I just wanted to share it with a little soul who didn't have love but needed it so badly.

And you know what's funny. That year of being a room mom felt like a total disaster to me. The other room moms made all their treats. I bought mine. They crafted all these cute things for their class. I bought mine, usually the night before. I felt rushed coming from work to classroom parties. But my son still talks about how much he loved me being a room mom. He told me all the kids in his class loved me and that me signing up to be a room mom when no one else did was one of the coolest things about me. So when they say that kids just want you to show up, I guess that really is true!

Now, let's address the even larger adoption elephant in the room—that fear we bury so deep in our hearts that we can't even admit it to ourselves. "What if I can't or don't attach with this child?" This is a fear all mommas—adoptive and non-adoptive alike—have.

> Let's address the even larger adoption *elephant in the room*. "What if I *can't or don't attach* with this child?"

For me, this fear was even bigger when we started the adoption process because I already had a biological child. The reason for this fear, though, is probably not what you are thinking. I didn't fear that I wouldn't attach to this new child as well as I did my biological son. I feared that this new child would attach more to my husband than to me. Again.

Remember how I told you I was a working mom? Not just a working mom, I was a traveling mom. I would be gone for a few days at a time, sometimes a week or more, and Jeremy would be at home with Clyde all by himself—single dad-ing it up. At the time, he only worked Tuesdays, Thursdays, and Sundays, so they had a lot of time together. On the days Jeremy did go into work at the church, Clyde went with him for Mother's Day Out. He actually did the math one time, and he spent something like 85 percent of his waking time with Clyde.

My dream of having a momma's boy wasn't a reality for me at that time. I mean, don't get me wrong, he wasn't repulsed by me. We did have a good relationship, and I was a good mom. I just didn't get the one-on-one time with Clyde that my husband did. And it still stung when we walked into a room of strangers, and Clyde wanted Dad and not Mom.

So going into this adoption, fear absolutely gripped my heart that this little boy was going to love his dad more than me, too. This, I told myself, would finally prove I wasn't a good enough mom.

Jeremy literally began praying, unbeknownst to me, that this little boy would be obsessed with me.

This was a reminder to be careful what you pray for moment,

because the first few months, our little 8-month-old Nate would not let me put him down and only asked for Momma. Middle grounds can be nice, too.

I am not saying that attachment is always immediate, especially when you are talking about kids in different age groups and those coming from diverse backgrounds. I know many mommas for whom attachment was a much longer process that required patience and hard work. They had to prove their love to their child before they could let their guard down and trust that this was really their forever home.

But I share my experience because I want you to know you are not the only momma with this fear. I also want you to know that our God is faithful. I promise you, sweet friend, that if God gave you even the smallest push toward adoption, you can ignore that chatter that says you are not good enough. Ignore that lie that says there's no way you can bond with a child who did not grow inside of you. You are God's child, and that is enough.

Chapter 7:
Choosing Your Agency is Like Choosing Your Hairstyle

I have a dirty little secret to share.

I LOVE Mary-Kate and Ashley Olsen. We are about the same age, so in a way, I grew up with them. They were my style icons. Don't get me wrong, I still love keeping up with them and their bag lady, older man dating/marrying ways, but in my adolescent and teen years, they were at the pinnacle of the boho chic trend. I was the first to buy their Walmart brand clothes, platform flip-flops, and signature hair clips and scarfs. And you better believe we bought all of their straight-to-DVD movies. All of them.

About the time their movie "Billboard Dad" was released (I am throwing it way back here), they had these cute, flippy, bob haircuts. Their hair was short, but they styled it oh-so-cute. It was *the* haircut to have.

So, naturally, my younger sister and I both wanted to sport the do. My favorite Olsen twin was Ashley and hers was Mary-Kate. So my mom decided to take us to this new, very trendy, very expensive salon that came recommended by a family member. This was a huge treat, as we did not usually spend this much on our hair. We each walked in to the hair stylist with our picture of the Olsen twin cut that we wanted—two very different styles. We were so excited.

Well, guess what! This very expensive, highly recommended stylist SWITCHED OUR HAIRCUTS. I got the Mary-Kate! Mind you, the Mary-Kate was much shorter than the Ashley cut. I was in 7th grade at the time, fresh with braces, and a very, very short bob that flipped out at the end, which made me look like Lisa Rinna. Not that there is anything wrong with looking like Lisa Rinna now, but when you are in the 7th grade, you don't want to look like Lisa Rinna. You want to look like Ashley Olsen.

There is still photographic evidence of this floating around my parents' house. And every time we stumble upon this picture, my sister cracks up laughing and says how thankful she is to this day she got the Ashley. Maybe there is a deep-seeded, psychological reason I wear my hair so long these days.

However, that experience is why I liken choosing your adoption agency to choosing your hairstyle. Sure, you can make a change if you don't like your choice, but it can be a lengthy and painful process that might make you lose a lot of time, potentially money, and force you to revisit previously completed requirements and paperwork.

There are four very important factors you can control in the beginning stages of the adoption process:

1. Choosing Your Adoption Agency

2. Can I Parent This Child?/Children's Needs Questionnaire

3. Dear Case Manager Letter

4. Your Family Book

Choosing your adoption agency is your number one priority and should not be taken lightly. These people will prepare you for your family changes, advocate for you when you submit your home study, encourage you during the process, and help you after placement. Here are some things you want to look for in your agency:

- Experience with CPS
- Counseling services
- Post adoption services
- Support groups
- General adoption resources
- Policies & Ethics: Many agencies require one parent to be a stay-at-home parent, so for us, that just wouldn't work. Some agencies have minimum salary requirements and more. So just make sure you meet all requirements before applying.
- Proximity of the office to your home: You will be spending a lot of time here for classes, looking at profiles, etc.
- References: I would ask for one family who has completed their adoption and one family who's adoption is in-process.

For us, choosing an agency with Christian values was just as important as these practical considerations. It was so amazing to be able to share our Christian values and pray with our agency during the process. There are so many times when you need a cheerleader and someone to speak biblical truths in your life while fighting for a child to come into your family. I know I could not have made it through the two and a half years without our case manager being that person.

When we were choosing an agency, we were very fortunate to attend a Wait No More seminar put on by a collaboration of Focus on the Family, Houston DFPS (Department of Family and Protective Services), adoption agencies, church leaders, and ministry partners. The seminar was meant to raise awareness about children who need families and to recruit families for children within the church community. How rare is it to see the church and the State come together? This signifies there MUST be a dire need.

After the conference, we attended a fair to meet all the agencies in Houston, talk to a representative from each, and take home their information.

We took information packets from every single booth, and then we went on a lunch date to our favorite downtown restaurant from our pre-kid days, laid out all the materials, and then started narrowing down agencies. We took something a little stressful and overwhelming, and we turned it into a date—full of fun, laughter, and just time to talk with each other. Honestly, it was such a special and sweet day together that I felt God had carved out especially for us to let us know this was the path He wanted us on.

For us, choosing our agency was a pretty quick and easy decision that felt very natural.

I had actually been familiar with our agency since I was a child because every year my church would collect shoes for one of the agency's ministries. The agency spends a lot of time and resources on this ministry, which sends shoes to orphans and vulnerable children around the world who walk miles and miles to school and work with no shoes. We also knew a couple who took mission trips with the agency to distribute shoes and minister to different villages all over the world.

How cool is it that God pulled on my little heart, even then, to love orphans?

God had a heart for the orphans and the widows. The Bible actually has 27 verses about orphans and 31 verses about widows. Anytime the Bible references something multiple times, it means that is important and dear to God's heart, something to be taken seriously in our personal lives. A love of and passion for taking care of the vulnerable was priority one for us in an agency.

We wanted to be aligned with an agency who took this charge to heart and addressed these needs fully.

> God had a **heart** for the **orphans** and the widows. The Bible actually has *17* **verses** about orphans and 31 verses about widows.

One factor that initially drew us to our agency was their full range of services for families—not just adoption. Our agency also offers retirement services with beautiful senior living facilities, assisted living, mental health care, and even hospice care. They have family centers that provide services and support to strengthen families. One of my favorite services our agency offers is a program that helps single parents. They assist with education, housing, and tools and skills to help the family succeed. Our agency truly puts their money where their mouth is with this program, loving on the family, the mom, and the children. And they are an independent charity to boot!

All of these programs that drew us to our agency were just bonuses. They showed us the heart of the organization. But on top of just loving God and loving children, our agency is a large, professional organization that offers many practical, helpful adoption services, including:

Education and Training

- Webinars
- Book reviews, videos, and resources on their blog

Counseling Services

- Consultation, providing information and resources
- Referrals to services
- Coaching through challenges
- Support groups (remember how important I told you this was?)
- Clinical counseling with a licensed professional
- Attachment assessments to help you understand your attachment style

Post-Adoption Services

For adoptive parents:

- De-identified copies of your child's adoption record
- Search assistance to obtain medical information
- Search assistance to open a closed adoption
- Ongoing training and education opportunities
- Post adoption counseling services

For adoptees:

- De-identified copies of your adoption record
- Listing in the Mutual Consent Adoption Registry
- Search assistance in finding birth parents
- Post adoption counseling services

For birth parents:

- Background history search for adopted children
- Listing in the Mutual Consent Adoption Registry
- Search assistance in finding birth children
- Post adoption counseling services
- Assistance in updating your birth child's file

Adoption is a major life event. For the parents. For the children. And no matter how much our family loves each other, adoption always comes with a loss that can hit at different stages of life.

I cannot stress to you the importance of finding an agency that provides these things! The whole process can be so difficult emotionally— waiting, attaching, dealing with trauma, coping with loss. These can be life-long struggles. You want to make sure you have a real partner and resource to turn to.

And do not think that just because you adopt an infant you won't ever need these services. You never know what (or at what stage) your child may go through these challenges. Adoption can especially be difficult in those teenage years when identity is already a hard thing to find. Having having an agency that provides training, support, and counseling should be a requirement for all adoptive parents.

Our agency has been such a blessing to my whole family. We have been off of their official docket as a foster and adoptive family for over a year now, since we finalized Nathaniel's adoption, but they are still a constant presence in our life. For one thing, after we finalized our adoption, Nathaniel was diagnosed with chronic asthma, as well as some other medical issues. They continue to provide services, consultation, and pointed us in the right direction as to how we could apply for subsidies. This support has been so helpful and comforting in a time of so much stress.

Our agency's chapter in Houston is just amazing. For Christmas, they sent our family an invitation for their Polar Express Christmas party. Again, Nathaniel had already been adopted at this point. The invitation was not your standard mail invitation; it was a large gift basket FedExed to our home. In the basket, we received a matching pair of PJs (in the boys' correct sizes) for Nathaniel and for Clyde, a copy of the "Polar Express" book, four coffee mugs, a pair of Christmas socks for my husband and me, a train ticket to their Polar Express, and two believe bells. It was amazing!

The boys were so excited.

The party was even more fabulous! They had a pancake breakfast, coffee food truck, the "Polar Express" movie playing, and Santa even came out to give each child (even the bio children) a personalized gift. It was so magical and special. My boys loved it!

We have even made friends with several families who were either in our classes at the same time we were, or we have met along the way. The bond that forms from seeing our new families grow together is so special and such a blessing.

Our agency also offers a (free!) camp every summer for foster, foster-to-adopt, and adoptive families. This free getaway is a great time to be with your family and connect with other families who are going through or have been through what you have. It is also beneficial for your kids to see other families similar to your own. I cannot wait to attend next summer!

Hopefully you see why I think your agency is such an important decision. Our agency did not just help us find our child, which is a huge responsibility in and of itself, but they are a lifelong friend and partner.

And by the way, I do not work for our agency, and I am in no way paid by them to promote them. I just love them that much! I want you to find an agency that you feel this passionately about, as well, because they become a part of your growing family.

Chapter 8:
The Matching is the Hardest Part

As far as our story goes, I am glossing over the part about classes and training for now. There are a lot of classes and requirements, all of which I will address in the second half of the book. This process is long and tiring, but it is important for preparing you and your family for what is to come.

I thought that waiting was going to be the most difficult part of the adoption process for me. Especially because that time period was extremely difficult for me wanting a child so badly and having only that desire to hold onto during the silence. But I was so, so wrong. I was unaware of how local adoption works. I always had this notion, especially since I really only ever considered international adoption, that you saw a cute face online, you did a ton of paperwork, you met them in person, and you brought them home. Bam. Done.

Well, that is not quite how it works with adoption through CPS. In the very beginning of the paperwork process, you fill out a very long and detailed profile on what you are looking for in a child and what special needs you would be willing to take on. I mean, this questionnaire is so detailed it even asks you minor things such as: Would you be willing to have a child who is cross-eyed—check yes or no. Why is that even a question? I have to tell you—this was very hard to complete. You really need to spend a lot of time on this in prayer with your spouse, as this profile becomes the most important piece of paper when it comes time to match with ready children.

I included a sample of what this questionnaire looks like in the resource section on page 192. I suggest you begin praying over this now. Whether you are looking at domestic or international adoption, you need to be realistic about what kind of child you can parent and what kinds of special needs you can meet.

I don't know about you, but I feel like there are some pretty detailed questions here. I mean, you don't have to fill this out when you are pregnant and tell your doctor, "Um I want a boy, I want him to be completely healthy, an innie belly button, or no deal. You can just swap him with another baby!" Ha. But that is exactly what I felt like I was saying when I completed this form.

However, there is so much more on this sheet for you to consider—learning disabilities, emotional needs, and physical challenges. There are even diseases, that maybe you had never even thought about, to consider. If you're pursuing domestic, CPS adoption, once you fill this out and have a license from the state, your agency case manager will notify you of children who are eligible to be adopted. They read to you a child's profile as given to them by the CPS broadcast. You have anywhere from two days to two weeks, depending on the deadline, to decide if you would like to submit your home study to "apply" for this child. And if you have questions, you're somewhat out of luck. You are really only given the file in front of you.

This profile will include a picture of the child (or children if you applying for sibling sets) and basic information such as the child's eating and sleeping habits, activities, developmental progress, and behavior. It will also contain some background information on the birth family, how the child came into care, and any known medical issues. This profile, as we discovered, is compiled from monthly updates as given by the foster parents.

This profile contains private, sensitive information. For that reason, your agency will not let you make copies, and they cannot email you this information. Your case manager will call you over the phone and read you the contents of the file. Even though our case manager would call us and read the details, I would drive 90 minutes to the office just to be able to read the file and take my time digesting all the information.

Word to the wise: Read between the lines and use cautionary judgment. For example, we were only looking at children under the age of two, and every profile we read said that they slept through the night. Um, yeah, okay. So if a profile says mild behavior in young children, I would probably read that to be more severe.

These profiles certainly include facts about the child, but they are also put together with the mindset of wanting the child to have a forever family. I would compare this to your Instagram profile. You are only posting your best photos and telling the story of your family that you want people to see. You are not lying; you are just presenting yourself in the best possible light. You may even throw your followers a bone every now-and-again and post one of those "real life moments." You know, the one where you're just waking up, your hair and makeup undone, and you find your kids have destroyed your downstairs. You know, that kind of post? That is how I like to think of these profiles. Truth in a marketing sense.

This stage is where that questionnaire I was telling you about (page 192) comes into play. If I were to do this process again, I would make a copy of that questionnaire (the one where we noted what we can and can't handle), hang it on my fridge, and consult it each time we made the decision to submit our home study for a child. This part of the process was the most grueling and heart wrenching for me, and I was totally unprepared for those feelings. Once I saw photos of these children, they were not hypothetical anymore. I was looking at them and praying, "Is this my son?"

We were so excited and hopeful for the very first boy we submitted our home study for. We knew that our target profile, males under the age of two and no sibling groups, was the most sought-after group. But what that actually meant, we had no idea, was that more than 150 home studies were submitted for this one little boy.

Once all the home studies are received, they are reviewed by that child's CPS case manager and supervisor, and the top three families are chosen. Those three families' agency case managers then sit in front a committee in what is called a RAS (Review Approval Screening) meeting.

/noun/ ras meet·ing

'ras mēdiNG:

When a child in the foster care system needs to be placed in a permanent home, a committee made up of the child's CPS case manager, CPS supervisor, and the child's CASA worker comes together. The profiles of the top three families are chosen, and a rep for each of the three families advocates for them at the RAS meeting. The selection committee chooses one of the three to parent the child.

The advocate for each family argues why they would be a good fit and shows off the families' book (I have an example of our family book in the next section!). The board then convenes and chooses which family the child will be placed with.

We were one of the three families chosen out of more than 150 to attend the RAS Meeting for the first child we applied for; we couldn't believe it! We received the call about his profile just a week after we had our license. We had to wait a couple of weeks for the meeting, and we were trying to not get our hopes up, but secretly, we were so excited and thought that, of course, we would be chosen. How could we not? It must be fate, we thought, that we had received this call so fast. We are a happy family with a solid support system.

Well, we weren't chosen. We were told we "tied for first." Um, no that's called losing. We did NOT have a child placed in our home at this time.

This little 2-year-old boy had experienced some major abuse from his biological father, and he was scared of men. Since I work full time and my husband works part time, he is actually home more with the kids. The committee thought that might be a problem. Also, since the little boy was Hispanic, he was placed with an adoptive father who was Hispanic, so he would have a little more of a cultural tie.

I logically understood why this decision was made. We, of course, want what is best for that child. But that day, I was crushed. I wanted to be his momma. I already fell in love with him and his little picture. I already imagined him being a part of my life and me taking care of him, rocking him, dressing him, wiping his tears away, and kissing him. I felt like I lost my son.

We all, my whole extended family, were attached to the idea of this little boy coming into our home, as well. So after our first RAS rejection, we decided we would not tell our families about the children unless we were chosen for the top three. It was just too emotional.

We applied for nine more children before being matched.

We also looked at profiles for two other children who, with the heaviest hearts, we could not apply for. Not applying for these beautiful children felt almost as bad as us not being matched. I felt like these little boys were standing in front of me, and I was personally rejecting them. We knew that the care they needed was beyond our scope as parents at that time, but that didn't mean I wasn't honestly heart broken. The thought of saying "no" to those children still haunts me to this day.

Like I said, matching was the hardest part of the process. And I had no idea. I was so under prepared. Even knowing that now and being as prepared as possible, I think it would still be extremely hard.

After the ninth child we had calls with our agency about, the process started to really take an emotional toll on us. I told my husband that I just couldn't go into the agency office, look at these detailed profiles, see their sweet faces, and stress and worry over each child. I decided to distance myself a bit and trust our agency to only send us children who met our profile. Then, we would just take a leap of faith.

The decision to release the "control" I felt I had in the process was monumental.

And after making it, we received a call about a little boy who needed to be moved from a foster-only home to a permanent home. CPS was in the legal process of changing his plan to non-related permanent adoption and moving to terminate parental rights. He was seven months old and had no medical or emotional issues. He was very loving, enjoyed eating, and of course, slept through the night (wink, wink). I'm obviously giving you the abridged version of his profile, as the file goes into all the case details. But for us, everything on the surface checked out and matched our requirements.

We decided, over the phone, that we would go ahead and submit our home study to be considered, and we wouldn't come into the office to parse the file. We were chosen for the RAS for a second time. Thankfully for us, this was the last time we were chosen for a RAS meeting. We were matched with our son.

If I can give you one more piece of advice, it would be to keep a journal during this time. Only God can write these beautiful stories. I'm amazed how God shows up clearly to make His Glory known. He wrote this story, not us.

Pray, pray, and pray more during this time. Lean into your spouse, and don't let this come between the two of you. Let it make you stronger and depend on God for strength during this time.

Notes

PART THREE
Starting the Adoption Process

"God has your child, your specific, beautiful child, waiting for you. His timing doesn't always match ours, but it's so much more beautiful that way.

Chapter 9:

Inquiry and Pre-Application

The second half of the book I want to spend with you going into detail about what the adoption process entails and what you can expect. I can't tell you what is going to happen in between various stages of the process or give you exact timelines—the world of adoption is an uncertain one. But just so you know—so is motherhood in general. Just like if you had a dozen pregnancies, if you had a dozen adoptions, they would all be different. But don't let that uncertainty scare you! Instead, replace that fear by equipping yourself with truths and knowledge of the process so you have a general idea of where you are headed and what is required to navigate the process.

If you have made it this far in the book, I assume you have bought into the idea of adoption in general. Maybe you and your spouse have even come together and jointly, definitively decided you want to add to your family through adoption. Now you just have to decide what type of adoption you want to pursue and apply to the program in which you would like to participate.

Here's the crazy, surprising part: You actually must get accepted into the program and agency for which you are applying. This is one point that most people who ask us for a broad overview about our adoption are surprised to hear. We get pretty much the same reaction every time: "Wow,

I had no idea you had to be accepted first to even begin the process."

To tell you the truth, I didn't really either. And as I mentioned earlier, we did not get accepted into the first program we applied for, which made the disappointment that much greater and really threw me for a loop.

We originally choose our agency and the domestic infant adoption program purely because we knew someone who had adopted their child from that agency and program years before. Here I was all set to start the process. I was ready to go. I thought by putting in my "pre" application, I was on the road to adopting! We even had our adoption announcement made and announced it to the world via Facebook. Once you make it Facebook official, there's no turning back, right?

All of a sudden, we weren't accepted into the program, and we didn't know of any other agencies. We didn't know where to turn. We felt like we had been stopped before we even started.

But God knew what He was doing. This roadblock allowed me to learn about all types of adoption—specific programs and their different requirements.

Domestic Infant Adoption	Foster-to-Adopt
Overview Domestic infant adoption involves the prospective adoptive family working with an agency to prepare a home study and portfolio for pregnant birth mothers to review as they choose an adoptive family for their child.	The foster-to-adopt program is unique within the State foster care system. Foster parents agree to care for a child in the hopes of adopting the child if and when parental rights are terminated.
Cost $25,000 to $35,000	Attorney fees that will be reimbursed after finalization
Challenges The birth mom chooses the parents for her child. Typically the birth mother has 48 to 72 hours after birth to change her mind. Some states even follow the Uniform Adoption Act allowing a mother up to eight days to change her mind.	The majority of these children have come into State care through CPS because of some level of neglect or abuse. The birth parents have one year to work through that plan. If the birth family completes the requirements in this plan, the child can be reunited with their biological family.
Benefits You have the child since birth, and you get to experience the infant stage. Potential for a semi-open or open adoption with the birth mother. This can be very beneficial for the child in the long run for feeling connections to their birth family.	Many families have zero expenses related to the adoption. There are also monthly subsidies during the foster period, and there are potential subsidies after adoption for health care, Medicaid, and possibly state college tuition.

Domestic Waiting Child	International Adoption
Overview Waiting children or "legally free" children are children in the State's CPS program who are currently in foster homes. The court has terminated the parental rights of both birth parents and all appeals have been exhausted.	International adoption is similar to domestic adoption in the fact that both programs are working toward the same legal goal of transferring parental rights to the adoptive parents.
Cost Attorney fees that will be reimbursed after finalization	$25,000 to $45,000 depending on country and agency
Challenges These children are typically part of sibling sets and are often five years of age and older. The majority of these children have come into state care through CPS because of some level of neglect or abuse.	Rules and regulations vary from country to country. There are also additional challenges to working with another country's government, so it can be difficult to ensure ethical standards are being followed. This is why agency scrutiny and knowledge of adoption rules and regulations from the country you are adopting from is key.
Benefits This can definitely be a faster route to adoption, and you also don't have to jump through all the hoops of being a foster parent. There is also very little cost and potential for adoption subsidy and free, state college tuition for some children.	You do not have the lengthy time of being a foster parent or have to face the uncertainty of birthparents. There are a lot of children available worldwide that vary from different ages, boy and girls, and many different countries all over the World.

Selecting an Agency and Adoption Program

1) Domestic Infant Adoption

Many first time adoptive families start out wanting to adopt an infant. Infant adoption is the most sought-after, and therefore, the most difficult placement to find. I was right there with you! This is where we started our adoption story, as well, although we did not end there.

Domestic infant adoption involves the prospective adoptive family working with an agency to prepare a home study and portfolio for pregnant birth mothers to review as they choose an adoptive family for their child.

It is common for birth parent(s) to want to get to know the adoptive family a little better. Today, most adoption professionals encourage an "open adoption" because it helps the birth mother feel more confident in the family she's chosen and for the life she has envisioned for her child, as well as helping the child feel more secure and connected.

/noun/ o•pen a•dop•tion

ōpən əˈdäpSII(ə)n:

"Also known as a cooperative adoption, this type of adoption allows for some form of association between the birth family, adoptees, and adoptive parents. This can range from picture and letter sharing, to phone calls, to contact through an intermediary, to open contact between the parties themselves. Many adoptions of older children and teens are at least partially open, since the children may know identifying or contact information about members of their birth families or may want to stay in touch with siblings placed separately.

An open adoption agreement spells out the terms of the contact between the parties in an open adoption. An open adoption agreement can specify frequency and manner of contact between adoptive and birth families and/or between siblings placed separately."[4] So you would know what level of "open" you would be looking towards and what you would be willing to commit to.

Birth mothers can change their minds about adoption until they sign the legal paperwork. Typically the birth mother has 48 to 72 hours after birth to change her mind. However, each state varies on the time frame they offer a birth mother to sign her paperwork. Some states even follow the Uniform Adoption Act[5] allowing a mother up to eight days to change her

---

4 Adopt.org/glossary
5 Family-Law.FreeAdvice.com/family-law/adoption_law/reverse_adoption.htm

mind. So you will definitely want to check out what your state laws are.

Most domestic infant adoptions cost between $25,000 and $35,000. The reason for this high cost is that you, the adoptive family, pay for the birth mom's medical expenses (our medical expenses for our biological son were in the range of $7,000 to $10,000 with insurance) as well as agency and legal fees.

What does an open adoption actually mean?

There is not one definition for open adoption as every situation is different. The level of communication in an open adoption depends on your agency and the agreement they have with the birth mother. These arrangements can be as simple as sending a package to the birth mother once a year until the child turns five, or they can look more like having regular calls, emails, or visits.

Some agencies will even offer semi-open adoptions where all communications are mediated through adoption professionals, and there is no exchange of personal information.

You need to decide your comfort level when it comes to the openness of your adoption prior to choosing your agency.

2) Foster-to-Adopt through CPS

The foster-to-adopt program is unique within the State foster care system. Foster parents agree to care for a child in the hopes of adopting the child if and when parental rights are terminated. The majority of these children have come into state care through CPS because of some level of neglect or abuse.

Your adoption agency works alongside State social workers to place the child in your home. While the child is in your home, the State/CPS works concurrently with the child's biological family on what's called a family plan of reunification.

/noun/ re•u•ni•fi•ca•tion

rē yōonifə'kāSH(ə)n:

"Occurs when a child who has been in foster care returns to his or her birth family. Reunification is the goal for many children in foster care."[6]

The birth parents have one year to work through that plan. If the birth family completes the requirements in this plan, the child can be reunited with their biological family.

But once it looks like reunification will not be possible, the foster-

---

6 *Adopt.org/glossary*

to-adopt family is in place to adopt the child.

As a foster-to-adopt parent, even though your ultimate goal is adoption, your home must be licensed by the State as a foster home. You will have the same requirements as a foster family, which include additional classes than Waiting Texas Children families would be required to take—and you will have monthly visits from your agency, your social worker, any therapy or doctor's appointments that the State has deemed necessary for the child, and potentially a CASA worker.

While your home is under foster status, the family receives benefits from the State, which vary among states, but typically includes:

- Monthly reimbursements
- Medical assistance
- Social services
- A one-time-only reimbursement of non-recurring adoption expenses such as lawyer fees to complete the adoption.

If the State designates the child as "special needs," some of these benefits may continue after your adoption is finalized.

Of course, there is always the potential of a child's reunification with the birth family and adoption no longer being an option. But this is typically the best route if you are looking to adopt a child under the age of two. This plan can also be called "legal-risk" adoption since there is a greater risk of an adoption not being completed due to reunification with their birth family.

This program was created to bridge the gap of children being placed in multiple homes during the foster care and adoption process. Typically, children are moved from foster homes to foster-to-adopt homes once the child's plan has changed from "reunification" to "unrelated adoption" to make the transition smoother if parental rights are terminated.

/noun/ un·re·lat·ed a·dop·tion

ənrəlādəd ə'däpSII(ə)n:

Unrelated adoption is a term used in the adoption world to signify that the goal of adoption has been changed from reunification with the birth family and that all other related family members have been exhausted, so CPS will now look to place the child in an unrelated foster home.

What children are considered "special needs?"

In State (foster care) adoptions, this definition can apply to most of the children in care—so do not let this term necessarily deter you! This wording is used to define state laws, eligibility for federal financial assistance, but it is not necessarily indicative of the traditional form of mental and physical disabilities and "special needs," though it absolutely can be.

If the child has any one of the following, they are classified as "special needs" by DFPS:

- Minorities/ethnic or racial background
- Age (many programs define this as children over the age of six)
- Sibling groups
- Diagnosed medical, physical, or emotional disabilities
- Risk of physical, mental, or emotional disability based on birth family history
- Any condition that makes it more difficult to find an adoptive family

Again, check with your specific state for the definitive definition and parameters.

3) Domestic Waiting Child

Waiting children or "legally free" children are children in the State's CPS program who are currently in foster homes. The court has terminated the parental rights of both birth parents and all appeals have been exhausted.

These children are typically part of sibling sets and are often five years of age and older. This can definitely be a faster route to adoption, and you also don't have to jump through all the hoops of being a foster parent.

However, with this program, you do not receive monthly reimbursement and subsidy advantages like you would with the foster care subsidy, unless they are eligible for the special needs subsidy. Again, this varies by state so definitely check with your agency.

/noun/ **fos•ter care sub•si•dy**

fôstər ker səbsədē:

DFPS provides assistance and financial reimbursement to foster families. Check with your state to determine the rate specific to your state's program.

/noun/ **spe•cial care sub•si•dy**

speSHəl nēdz səbsədē:

The Special Care / Special Needs Subsidy is available to parents even after adoption through CPS for children with designated special needs that require medical assistance, child care, and/or special equipment. Check with your state to determine the rate specific to your state's program.

As with children in the foster-to-adopt program, the agency typically does not charge anything to adopt waiting children. Usually your only costs associated with a waiting child adoption are minimal legal fees.

4) International Adoption

International adoption, in my opinion, can be the most complex type of adoption. Rules and regulations vary from country to country. There are a lot of agencies that claim to have experience they don't have or those that do not always follow through. But sometimes, they are also limited by communication from the country's government they are working within.

International adoption is similar to domestic adoption in the fact that both programs are working toward the same legal goal of transferring parental rights to the adoptive parents. International adoption varies in the legal process and amount of paperwork required to make the adoption happen.

Make sure your agency has experience with the country from which you want to adopt. Do not be shy to ask for references of families who have been through the process both successfully and unsuccessfully.

International adoption usually costs anywhere between $25,000 to

$45,000 depending on the country and your agency. Many of these fees are dictated by the international country and consist of a lot of legal fees and travel costs.

What is the Hague Convention?

The Hague Convention was created to establish a baseline of standards for international adoptions. Not all countries have agreed to be part of this, so countries within the convention have more protection than countries outside the convention. You can find a list of countries that participate with the Hague Convention at: Travel.State.gov/content/adoptionsabroad/en/hague-convention/convention-countries.html

Adoption Consultants

I wanted to add a little note about considering using an adoption consultant for infant and international adoption. An adoption consulting agency is made up of experienced professionals, many of whom have adopted themselves, who provide you with an extra layer of financial advice, education, and guidance, and who serve as a personal advocate for you.

Now, you may say to yourself, isn't that what I am using an agency for? Yes, but consultancies also offer potentially shorter wait times and networking among multiple agencies, and they help you create your profile book and paperwork. Yes, consultants add an additional cost, but they offer a range of packages for their services. Plus, the ability to work with multiple agencies and assistance with international paperwork can be a huge added value. Hiring a consultant is certainly not necessary, but it could be worth looking into for your family.

Costs

A couple of these adoption options have a large price tag attached. Many people I talk to are outraged at the sound of this. But keep in mind: There are a lot of legal fees and travel included in these costs. Not to mention, just to keep things in perspective for you, that according to "USA Today," the average cost of a car in the United States has price tag of $33,560.[7] And not only do we pay that much for vehicles, but according to U.S. Department of Motor Vehicles, the average household has an average of 2.8 cars.[8] But aside from that, here are some ways to bring these costs down:

- There are many grants available to adoptive families. Just

    a do a Google search for "adoption grants," and you'll find

_____

7 USAToday.com/story/money/cars/2015/05/04/new-car-transaction-price-3-kbb-kelley-blue-book/26690191/

8 Rita.dot.gov/bts/sites/rita.dot.gov.bts/files/publications/highlights_of_the_2001_national_household_travel_survey/html/section_01.html

a lot of options.

- Check with your insurance provider and your employer. They may have programs that donate to your adoption— sometimes as much as $5,000.

- As of 2017, the adoption credit from the IRS had a maximum return of $13,570 per child. This is huge![9]

- Fundraising: "You Can Adopt Without Debt" is a great book by Julie Gumm with lots of helpful information and ideas on how to not go into debt with your adoption.

I know this is a lot of information and a variety of different programs. So I put together an overview chart of the different programs for you to compare the challenges and benefits to each at the end of the chapter.

Inquiry and General Application/ Pre-Application

Once you have spent time researching and praying over what program is the best fit for you as well as what agency can support you through this process, you can inquire with the agency and begin the general application

---

9 AdoptiveFamilies.com/resources/adoption-news/irs-increases-2017-adoption-tax-credit-maximum/

or pre-application. Many agencies offer information meetings to answer all of your questions, inform you of their programs, and give you the required paper work. The preliminary application is typically free and helps the adoption agency determine which program fits your family best. You can usually fill out these applications online or at the information meeting.

This is a great time to speak to your agency and get more information beyond what is on their website or brochures. Here are some good things to ask your potential agencies for:

- References from families who have adopted with them
- Their average wait time
- If they have any new programs to offer
- How long the program you are applying for has been open
- If they have any employee changes or any new policy changes that could affect the wait time or the process

Again, this is information you probably won't find online.

If the agency you are talking with doesn't want to provide you with this information or takes an unusually long time to respond, this is a very big red flag and probably means you need to move on to a different agency.

This pre-application is much more general and does not go into the amount of detail your formal application will. Once your pre-application is accepted, and you decide to move forward with the agency, a non-refundable deposit will be required to continue to the formal application for some agencies, especially for international adoption. This is a good way for the agency to make sure you are serious and committed about continuing the process before they add resources to further your adoption process.

Even if you are rejected from an agency or program, learn from my mistakes, and do not be alarmed, and do not be discouraged. A rejection does not necessarily have anything to do with you as a parent. It could be that you are too far from their location, you do not meet a requirement they have that other agencies might not necessarily have (being a stay-at-home mom, religious views, etc.), or in our case, the agency is not accepting new families into a specific program.

Going forward, I offer a lot of information from our personal experiences adopting through the domestic foster-to-adopt program. Some things may be slightly different for you depending on the program you choose. I will note what some of the differences could be and include information about various programs, not just adoption through CPS. However, as far as the overall process goes, 80 percent of the material should apply to everyone regardless of the program you choose.

Chapter 10:
Education and Formal Application

Education and formal application is a pretty significant portion of your adoption process. There are classes, webinars, and other potential trainings, such as CPR certificaitons, agencies will require you to take for most adoption programs.

So why do you need to take these classes, especially if you are already a parent? And even if you are not already a parent, you do not have to take classes to become a parent if you get pregnant, so why are these required?

These really are not so much parenting classes in the sense of teaching you how to be a parent. There are no diaper changing courses and/or suggestions of how to get accepted into Jessica Alba's all-organic, no-red-dyes-or-fast-food mom's club. (Just for the record, I totally was not accepted due to the amount of sweet tea and Chick-fil-A we consume.)

These classes equip you on how to parent a child who has experienced trauma, abuse, neglect, loss, as well as how to manage a blended family, cultural issues, etc. This is a different type of parenting at times than your approach to your biological children.

> These classes *equip you* on how to parent a child who has experienced *trauma*, *abuse*, *neglect*, *loss*, as well as how to manage a blended family, cultural issues, etc.

Again, every child is different, and the spectrum and level of issues resulting from trauma varies depending on age and their individual circumstances. But every child who enters a family via adoption has experienced trauma because they were seperated from their first family, so you want to be prepared to face these challenges (whenever they may appear) as much as possible before the child enters your home.

I know sometimes we view adoption as this perfect picture— we are going to meet this child, and they are immediately going to be so grateful and obsessed with us. Newsflash: Your biological kids don't/ wouldn't do that either. My 6-year-old does not wake up every morning and say, "Thank you mommy for having my clothes ready. And making me breakfast. And waking up before me so I can have a great day. Thanks for buying me groceries and working so I can have as many toys as Toys "R"

Us. You are my best friend."

Haha! It's more like this: "Mom, I hate this shirt! I don't like that breakfast! I don't want to wake up and go to school!" Now, of course, we have some very sweet times, as well. But the pictures we have of motherhood in general that are flawed. And with adoption there comes additional things that you could have to parent through.

These adoption training classes prepare you for these very possible realities.

One class that our agency had us take since we were adopting through CPS was called SAMA training, which stands for Satori Alternatives to Managing Aggression. I don't think this particular class is required by all agencies, as there are standards that all agencies have to comply with, but I think this was an extra class our agency felt parents who were fostering or adopting through the CPS system needed to take. SAMA was created to teach parents how to deal peacefully and correctly with children who display aggression.

They broke this training into two days. The first day we were in a classroom setting, learning how to communicate through tense situations. The second day was a day of physical training, learning techniques on how to block and deflect physical attacks and how to contain the child without harming them until they calm down (note: You legally may not be physical back to any child under CPS conservatorship).

/noun/ **c•p•s con•ser•va•tor•ship**

cps kən-sər-və-tər-ship:

"When a child must be removed from their home, the court appoints CPS to be a "conservator" of the child. That means CPS is legally responsible for the child's welfare and that is when a conservatorship (CVS) case worker comes in."[10]

Now let me just mention, we were only looking to adopt a child between the ages of zero and two, so we were probably not going to encounter many physical, aggression issues with the children we were applying to adopt, which is what made these SAMA classes my least favorite.

In the classroom, we had to role play different situations by following a formula of asking questions in a very specific way. Then we would act them out in a scenario in front of the class. I am not particularly fond of acting, and I especially do not like to role play in front of people I don't know, so this was a painfully awkward day for me.

But this role playing script did serve its purpose for us. "Daniel Tiger's Neighborhood" is a big deal at our house. We have watched every episode at least three times, and we have noticed that the adults use a

---

10 DFPS.state.tx.us/Jobs/CPS/cvs.asp

shortened version of the SAMA questioning technique when the children get upset. We would not have known that had we not taken this class. See, something sunk in and stuck!

Then, there was day two, the physical day on the mats. Number one: I am not physical, and I'm allergic to working out. So this is not fun for me. Number two: There were several moves that were very uncomfortable for people of the opposite sex to watch you do, getting taken down on the mat and such. And number three: There were several moves that you had to administer basically picking the other person up. Don't they know I can barely pick up my 3-year-old?! And please reference number one of me not working out.

So when we completed this class, I checked it off the list with pleasure and threw a little party that I had survived.

Now here is the truly ironic part of this story. This class is only good for one-year. So after we had Nathaniel in our home, the classes expired, and WE HAD TO TAKE THEM AGAIN. Seriously, if it wasn't for the whole you-can't-keep-your-son-if-you-don't-complete-this-class thing, there's no way I would have returned!

While this particular class was not my favorite, we took other classes that also tackle cultural issues, having a blended family, making sure you understand why you may need more cultural awareness, and put you in more diverse situations. These pre-adoption courses also prepare you for what the legal system looks like—both domestic and international.

I think one of the most helpful things discussed in these classes were the requirements that CPS has for you when you have a child in your home, since the State (CPS) is still the actual conservators of your child. There is absolutely no spanking or physical punishment allowed for children who are within the CPS system—zero tolerance policy.

There was a couple in our classes who had a young, biological son in their home already, when they decided to expand their family through the foster-to-adopt program. Physical punishment, in the context of spanking (not abuse), was a very, very sore point for the father. He believed strongly in the "spare the rod, spoil the child" verse in Proverbs 13:24.

And this father was not alone in his thinking; he was just the most vocal.

Bless our teacher. Just bless him. He had the patience of Gandhi himself. He was a Christian as well and knew the Scriptures intimately. He also had a lot of experience with children in CPS. The way he responded to this father's outrage was the best way I have ever heard someone explain why you can't spank these children.

First of all, your family is only held to CPS standards and rules while the child is still under CPS conservatorship. Once the adoption is finalized, the child is legally yours, and you are free to parent as you see fit. But more importantly, this rule was put into place for a very specific reason: These children are often coming from homes of neglect and abuse. Giving your biological child a spanking may signal to them that they need to stop what they are doing and correct their course. A spanking to a child who has experienced trauma could trigger their experience with and memories of actual abuse, potentially shattering any relationship you may have built with them to this point.

Once the father heard this explanation, he too changed his view on this rule. He understood why this was in place. Not just so some government entity could tell him how to parent, but rather to spare a child from further abuse and trauma. This is why we, as adoptive parents, go to these classes. We are learning about a whole new world and life we probably didn't know about or experience before.

This experience is also part of the reason for the SAMA classes—to show you alternative ways to this type of punishment and correction. So while SAMA classes weren't my favorite, they certainly served a very important purpose.

Your agency will most likely have a list of required classes and a schedule of when they are offered.

This is kind of like college. You can cram in as many classes as you want and go through them quickly like we did. Or you can schedule them at a more leisurely pace. And P.S. these are not short classes—most are eight-hour courses.

I personally recommend completing as many courses as you can as fast as possible. I know some couples use this training time as a dip-your-toes-in-the-water, just-see-what-you-think exercise. But I have often seen couples drag their feet during training and education, and then when they are finally ready to adopt, they are ready immediately and frustrated with the time they must invest in classes. Not to mention, many of these classes—not just the SAMA ones—are only valid for a year, so you might have to take them again the following year to keep your license open.

Formal Application

Once you complete a lot of these classes and have a better idea of the various programs and requirements, you can begin filling out the formal application. While each agency's application is going to ask different information, they will all require much more detail about your finances, your family set up, what exactly you are looking for in a child or sibling set, etc.

During this formal application process, you will also begin filling out the "Children's Needs Questionnaire." I know I have already talked about this as well as given you a sample copy of potential questionnaires in Chapter 16. However, I feel so strongly about the importance of this document that I want to mention it again.

This questionnaire is difficult to complete, and it will do you, and the child, no good to lie on this. This form is meant to help you and your case manager match you with a child. A child you have to parent. A child you have to love. A child who has to integrate into your life and your existing family unit. You need to be brutally honest with yourself and your spouse as to what type of child you can parent—temperament, physical needs, emotional needs, family history, trauma, abuse, race, you name it.

Now I know and believe there are things that God just changes your heart on during the process. Your life will change, and you must be more open—there is no doubt about that. God changed our whole heart to become foster-to-adopt parents when we initially had no desire to pursue that route. So believe me, I understand.

But there are some things that you may not want to bend on that can be really difficult when presented with a scenario. For us, we knew that we wanted a relatively healthy child under the age of two. We both work, so we knew we could not devote as much time as other families to major health or physical needs that may require extra attention. We also only wanted to accept one child in the home, not multiple children.

Our sweet case manager absolutely loved our family, our house, and our support system. He had the impossible task of trying to match our family, and he also had an incredible heart and passion for children.

He really encouraged us to consider opening our search parameters up to sibling sets. For one, there were more children who fell into this category. But he also truly loved our family and thought we were perfectly capable of parenting sibling sets and were the type of parents these kids needed.

However, when we started the process I had a 2½-year-old and was traveling about 30 percent of the time for work. So for me, personally, adding multiple children was just out of the question.

Our case manager on multiple occasions would say, "But are you sure?" I would remind him of why I felt like I couldn't parent that many kids at once, and he would always say, "I hear you, but I just think you are such great parents, you could handle it."

Two things would simultaneously happen to my psyche when he would tell me this. First, immense pride would swell up upon his compliment of my parenting. I would think, "I AM a great parent, aren't I?! I could totally parent multiple kids!" And then I would think about it and reality would set in about my work situation, my parenting abilities, and me in general. I mean, I can't even think about adding to my family in general until all children I currently have are potty trained. That is just how I work!

Then I would immediately start feeling guilty. "But there are children out there WHO NEED PARENTS. I am literally denying these children a home." Thoughts like this flooded my mind.

But then, I came back to this questionnaire that I had prayerfully and carefully completed. I came back to my husband and his part in the decision-making process. He, too, felt the way that I did in accepting only one child into our home. And then I returned to the truth and the calling God had laid out for our family, and I took comfort in knowing that He had this thing covered.

We also felt guilty on the two occasions we just had to say "no" to submitting our home study for children who were not quite in our parameters. One child had a looming health concern that we just weren't comfortable with handling well, and the other was due to their parental rights situation. I felt like a failure as a parent and felt that I was just being unwilling to help a child in need.

Sweet friend, don't make these big, life-changing decisions on your personal guilt. There are still going to be hundreds of thousands of children without homes. You have to be confident in the parents that you are and lean on God for direction and guidance, even if you are trying to be convinced otherwise. God has placed a calling in your heart. He will guide you, and He will lead you on the path He set out for you.

Chapter 11:
Screening Paperwork and Home Study

Once you reach the screening paperwork and the home study, you are starting to get down to the nitty gritty. It is pretty standard across the board that you will need to complete these items. This part of the process speaks to me because it involves a checklist—a list of things I know I have to get done that I can complete as I see fit!

Here is a general list of paperwork items required when adopting. This can obviously vary for each agency just like requirements for each state. But this will give you a good idea what is needed:

- Copy of valid driver's license
- Copy of GED, high school diploma, or other diploma
- Copy of marriage license, if married
- Physical evaluation for each adult in the home
- Tuberculosis screening for each family member (Check and see if a chest X-ray will suffice. This was a much better option for us, especially with little ones.)
- Floor plan of your home showing the dimensions of each room and what each room is used for
- Photos of exterior of your home

- Health inspection for home administered by the city

- Fire inspection for home and emergency evacuation plan for the home

- CPR certification for each adult in the home

- Copy of Social Security card

- Copy of current auto insurance

- Copy of current pet vaccinations, if you have pets

- Financial statements

- Photo of family (I suggest a professional photo. If you don't have one, now would be the perfect time to get those scheduled.)

- Copy of birth certificates

- For adoption finalization: Proof of medical insurance, proof of life insurance (Many agencies require a minimum of $50,000 per applicant.)

- A copy of will and contingency plan

- Three to five references

Your agency will also require a list of household items and safety considerations to be completed. A lot of these are requirements of the State, specific to foster or foster-to-adopt parents:

- First-aid kit

- Working carbon monoxide detector

- Working smoke detectors on every floor and near or in the child's room

- Medications, vitamins, cleaning products, other toxic substances out of child's reach (For foster parents, they must be double locked up.)

- Screen covering a fireplace or wood stove

- Covered kitchen trash

- Fire extinguisher near the cooking area of the home

- Covered outlets

- Gates for stairs

- Windows have secure screens and locks (There cannot be any holes in window screens. I promise they will check.)

- Household heating equipment has appropriate safeguards

- Fencing around swimming pool or pools of water

- Covering around any trampolines

- Locked tops on any hot tubs

- Emergency telephone numbers posted in the home

- Evacuation floor plans available

- Firearms in locked container with ammunition stored in a separate locked container

• No expired canned goods or medicine; food stored in the refrigerator must be marked with the date stored. (Again, this is one of the hot topic items, and they will check for this.)

Wow! Even looking at this now, this is quite a list—having to schedule appointments with inspectors, book health screenings, make copies of documents you may or may not have.

Plus, if you are going to be adopting internationally, you also need to complete the USCIS process and dossier, which can take even longer. There are many, many guides online about different dossiers specific to the country from which you are adopting. You definitely want to be familiar with this and have a great agency to walk you through this process.

/noun/ **u•s•c•i•s**

u-s-c-i-s:

"The U.S. Citizen and Immigration Services (USCIS) is responsible for:

• Determining the eligibility and suitability of the prospective adoptive parents (individuals) looking to adopt.

• Determining eligibility of the child to immigrate to the U.S."[11]

---

11 USCIS.gov/adoption

noun/ **dos•si•er**

dôsē,ā:

"A collection of papers containing very detailed information about you. The vast majority of countries open to international adoption require prospective adoptive parents to compile a dossier. Compiling a dossier involves gathering and notarizing documents and then adding various seals from your county, your state, and the U.S. government."[12]

Also, be aware that if you are going to be a foster or foster-to-adopt parent, any babysitter or family member that will be around your child or caring for your child under eight hours a week must complete a background check, fingerprinting, and CPR training. If someone will be watching your child more than eight hours a week or will be keeping your child overnight, they will need to be licensed for respite care.

/noun/ **res•pite care**

rē'spīt ker:

"Temporary care provided for a child in order to give the child's

---

12 Adopt.org/glossary

foster or adoptive parents time off or a rest from parenting."[13]

These caretakers must complete all the required training classes in addition to the above checklist (minus a home study) to provide this level of care. If your child will be attending a licensed daycare center or Mother's Day Out program, the workers there would not have to go through all of this because their facility is already licensed by the State.

These rules only exist while the child is in CPS conservatorship. Once the adoption is finalized, they are legally your child, and you no longer have to abide by these rules. But this is something definitely to consider when coming up with your child care plan.

We were so fortunate to have family members who completed the background check, finger printing, and CPR training so we could have some level of help with babysitters. But asking them to go through so many classes and that level of scrutiny to be licensed by the State was just too much for them! So a year later, once our adoption was finalized, we celebrated with a six-night cruise for my husband and me. It had been one year since we were child free overnight!

---

13 Adopt.org/glossary

Home Study

Once all of your classes are done and you complete all of the above checklist, you then get to move to the final stage of paperwork—the home study! Whether you decide to pursue foster care, domestic adoption, infant adoption, or international adoption, you'll have to complete a home study.

However, each home study is specifically tailored to each type of adoption. So if you change from infant adoption to foster-to-adopt, the home study may not transfer or may have to be altered with addendums.

Depending on your agency's capacity, this process can take three to six months to complete as they require very detailed documentation. The home study is a written document your case manager composes about your family, including basic information collected from interviews with your family (usually two visits that last three to four hours long) and information provided by third parties.

The home study typically includes:
- Family background, statements, and references
- Education and employment
- Relationships and social life
- Daily life routines
- Parenting experiences

- Details about your home and neighborhood

- Readiness and reasons for your desire to adopt

- Approval and recommendation of children your family can best parent

Again, this is why it is so important to pick the correct agency and have a case manager who is going to advocate for you. Your case manager is responsible for writing up your profile as a family. This profile will be looked at by your agency, other CPS workers, and any other agencies involved. The home study helps them match a child with you, so you want a writer who believes in you and your ability to parent. You also want to ask for a copy of your home study if they do not offer it to you so you can look over it and correct any inaccuracies.

If you are fostering or fostering to adopt through CPS, you probably will not have to pay a home study fee. However, if you are working with a private agency or a certified social worker in a private practice, the home study will cost you between $1,000 to $3,000.

You have probably already turned in the checklist of paperwork needed for your screening (the list I mentioned at the beginning of the chapter), but you will also want to have copies with you for the home study, as well. You will also have a list of items that need to be finished for your household requirements to be complete. Your case manager will be checking for them and writing about them during your home study.

Your case manager is not judging you on how Pinterest-worthy your house is and will not be checking underneath your couches with white gloves, looking for dust bunnies. They are checking to make sure your house is safe.

I don't know why, but I was really nervous for the home study. I suddenly felt like I was going on a job interview. But not just any job interview, no. A job interview critiquing my whole life, my home, and my ability to be a mother! Don't you know everyone is secretly scared to death about being *that* mom? The one their kids say drove them to therapy! I don't want a case manager making that determination this early on in my motherhood journey. Based on the many opinions and blog posts I have read online, I am not alone in this!

Honestly, the home study is simply a conversation between you, your family members, and your case manager detailing your family. If you have picked an agency you really like and feel comfortable with, this step will feel natural, and you will have no reason to be nervous.

At this point in our adoption process, we were working with an agency who was just opening, and we were one of the first families to go through the process. As a result of this, we felt like we got to know our case manager really well. Not to mention, he was just an incredibly kind man who genuinely liked people. The home study was the part of the process is where he shined the most because he really wanted to get to know our family. Again, the home study is so important in the matching process. Our family absolutely would not be knit together the way it is without our agency case manager.

I still remember the day our case manager came out to our house to conduct the home study. He was at our home for about four hours, and he said it could take an additional day of interviewing to complete. He had already come to know our family so well, however, so we completed the process relatively quickly. I know! A four-hour interview does not seem relatively quick.

During the home study conversations, the case manager must talk to all members of the household, including any children you have in the home, to ensure that everyone is on board and prepared. Clyde was just 2½ or 3 when we were at this stage, so there was obviously not a lot of deep questioning happening in those talks.

In fact, our case manager was so good that he simply went into our son's room (with us present as well, of course) and just played with him while having a conversation with him. Clyde was comfortable, in his own element, and did not feel like he was being interviewed.

We were applying for male children under the age of three with no race specified. So as our case manager is talking to Clyde, he cleverly asks him what he thought about children who were different than him or different races, without coming right out and saying that.

He asked Clyde, "If you could pick out any color hair for your new brother, what would you want it to be?"

Clyde thought really hard for a few seconds and as serious as he could be, he said, "Pink! I think that would be really cool."

I just love seeing the world through the eyes of children. They absolutely do not see things the way we do. They love more unconditionally, and heck, they are just more fun than we are. No wonder God knew that they would be our biggest gift and blessing. My heart has changed so much because of lessons that my children have taught me.

I was, however, a little surprised at the detail of all the questions in the home study. In fact, they closely resembled the questions we were asked during our eight-week premarital course. They asked questions about how both my husband and I were raised, including how discipline was administered in the home, what the family dynamic was, and how conflict was resolved.

They, of course, then asked a lot about present day adult life. What is your life like with your family and friends? What kind of support system do you have? What is your current work and financial situation? How do you cope with everyday stress, including any alcohol or drug dependency or history of such?

Your home study will dig into your marriage and ask about your ups and downs. Have you ever had to attend couples therapy, when and why? How do you make decisions together? Why do you want to adopt? What was your experience with and knowledge of the adoption process leading up to your journey? What is your arguing style?

A great deal of the home study will be spent on your parenting style. How will you handle conflict with your child? How will you introduce them to your life? What if people do not agree with your decision to adopt? Where will the child's room be? What will their childcare and extra curricular activities be? An even greater amount of time will be spent talking about interracial families and how you will make sure that the child is well-rounded, accepted, and made aware of his or her heritage.

And then, of course, if you have additional children in the home, great care will be taken to discuss how you will integrate all of your children into the process and educate them about adoption. Your case manager will also ask you about any potential conflict resulting from adding to your family unit and how you will respond to that, as well.

I think the key to a successful home study is preparing yourself and family members for these subjects and bracing yourself for the amount of detail you will be asked to go into. Just be honest, be yourself, and let the reasons you want to adopt shine through. And don't forget, it's just a conversation! You can ask questions, too.

Chapter 12:
Licensing

Obtaining a license from your state is only required for families who are fostering or fostering-to-adopt through CPS. However, this chapter isn't really about the requirements for your license. Those are addressed by the checklist in the previous chapter.

/noun/ **state li·cense**

stāt līs(ə)ns:

DFPS has a division for licensing that determines minimum care requirements. Child care facilities, respite care providers, and foster families must adhere to the rules and regulations of state licensing, must be inspected, and issued a license by the State before being able to accept children into the home for foster and foster-to-adopt.

Just to note: State-licensing requirements varies from state-to-state. A great place to check the requirements for your state is at AdoptUSKids.org.

This time period in between training and licensing for us was a time of waiting, and I want to talk about how it tested our faith tremendously.

After all of our classes were done, our home study had been completed, and all of our inspections were passed, we simply had to wait—and wait and wait and wait—for our license.

We actually entered our particular agency's branch when it first opened in our area, so we were one of the first families accepted into the program. This was great because we received even more personal attention than normal, and our paperwork and classes were pushed through quickly.

Then, our agency was flooded with kinship cases from CPS. These cases are priority because a child is already involved. So, our licensing by the State of Texas was the only thing we were missing. We had completed all of our paperwork, classes, health inspections, fire inspections, CPR training, and the home study interview, but our case manager had not finalized the home study to submit all of the paperwork to the State. We finished the home study in September and did not submit everything to the state until February.

/noun/ kin·ship a·dop·tion

kin,SHip ə'däpSH(ə)n:

Kinship adoption is when a family member pursues adoption of a relative, i.e. a niece, nephew, cousin, grandchild, etc. The laws for each state are very different, so visit Childwelfare.gov for laws applicable to your state.

Of course in this time of waiting, we had so many doubts. And by "we" I mean me. I am the worrier and feel like I have to control everything and take charge of the situation. My husband is much more patient, does not want to ruffle any feathers (his mantra is "fly under that radar"), and totally trusts in God's timing. But I especially hated the continual questioning by well-meaning friends and family asking for an update. Have I mentioned that? People asking me questions was obviously a very prickly subject for me at the time! And now here I am answering questions all the time.

I personally questioned over and over why this was taking so long because, the thing is, you cannot even start looking at children's profiles and begin submitting to be considered as their family until you have been issued a license by your state. In reality, this waiting period was only a few months, and this may happen in a totally different part of the process for you! But a few months seem like eternity when there is no movement, when there is nothing you can do to keep you busy.

We were finally licensed in February of 2014. Several more months later, we were matched and able to bring Nathaniel home.

When we were first given Nate's file from CPS, before placement, the incorrect date of birth was listed. Let that sink in for a moment. We were given our son's wrong birthday. He was actually a couple of weeks older than they told us. But you do not receive any official documentation until after you become their legal guardian.

So once that paperwork was processed, we were given a copy of his birth certificate. You can imagine our surprise at being told we were given the wrong birthdate. I mean, that is a pretty important piece of information!

But the real surprise came when we realized that Nate's actual birthdate was the exact same date we were licensed by the State of Texas.

> The real *surprise* came when we realized that Nate's *actual* birthdate was the *exact same day* we were licensed by the State.

God does not make mistakes. Here I was questioning this wait time. Questioning if God had really called us to this agency. Questioning if God really wanted us to adopt or if we had misunderstood. Questioning why

God would call us to this but then make us wait while we were getting older, Clyde was getting older, and I was trying to make our timeline fit in some perfectly planned box.

His timing did not match mine for a reason. We thought we had to wait too long to start our process. God was really preparing for us for what His plan already was. God knew—and obviously wanted to show us very clearly. He waited for that *exact* day to give us a very specific child. That is how intentional our God is.

Ecclesiastes 3:11 "He has made everything beautiful in its time. He has also set eternity in the human heart. Yet no one can fathom what God has done from beginning to end."

God has your child—your specific, beautiful child—waiting for you. His timing does not always match ours, but it is so much more beautiful that way. Don't lose heart! He always gives us what He promises.

A good thing to do during this waiting time is to begin working on your "Dear Case Manager" letter and your family book.

The Dear Case Manager letter is a one-page letter about your family, introducing yourself and your goals to the case manager who will be reviewing parents' applications and deciding how to permanently place a child. This letter is one of the first things that a case manager sees about your family, apart from your home study, and helps determine what three families they will choose to appear before the RAS committee. Note: If you are not adopting through CPS, you will not need to create this letter.

What I like about this process is that you can personalize the book yourself. In a system where so much is out of your hands, this is something you can control. And I love me some marketing materials, of course! Here are some items you want to include in your letter:

- A professional family photo
- Your profession
- Your family set up
- Social activities
- Why you want to adopt
- General scope of the child you are hoping to adopt and why

This letter is only one page, so you do not have much room for a ton of photos or even a lot of information. I also suggest you receive feedback from multiple professionals. Our case manager gave us his feedback and suggestions before he sent it to another agency location in another region for additional comments.

We received minor feedback about tweaking the letter with wording that would be attractive to a social worker. They suggested language like "bring a child into our home" or "our journey to be ready to bring another child into our home" versus "adopt."

We also thought that adding information about how we have always wanted to adopt internationally would be a plus, as our agency was impressed by this during our inital application. However, we received feedback to the contrary. Our advisers suggested that mention of future plans for international adoption may influence CPS staff to reconsider CPS adoptive placement in a home where there may be competing, possibly conflicting, goals of integrating a child from another country while a child placed through local adoption is also trying to adjust to the adoptive home.

Another piece of feedback we received was about the images we used. When I originally designed the letter, I added a family logo and other design elements I would add to any piece in my corporate, marketing world. Our case manager instead suggested we add a small photo our house or possibly even the playroom or back play area. The agency felt it may better present how child-friendly our home is.

Marketing professionals like yours truly surely know the value of focus groups and feedback! Details in the letter that I thought made our family stand out and look better were not necessarily in line with what a case manager looking to place a child wanted to see. These small suggestions and minor tweaks made a huge difference for us and helped elevate our letter to one that would not be passed up but would be read.

I have a sample of our letter for you to check out:

Dear Caseworker,

We would like to take the time to introduce ourselves as the James Family (Jeremy, Holly, and Clyde) and our journey to bringing another child into our family.

We (Holly and Jeremy James) were married on April 12, 2008 and have been married for 6 years. We had our 4-year-old son Clyde on July 13, 2010. We both have large extended families and share a love for the value of family and friends.

Jeremy James is Media Director for the The Bridge Fellowship. The Bridge recently launched a second campus at the Palladium Theater in Richmond, TX and Jeremy is part of the staff that stepped out. Holly James is Marketing Director for D&S Professional Services. We enjoy traveling, spending time with friends & family, church activities, comic books & legos!

Clyde is an intelligent, happy, healthy and very loved little boy. We have been very fortunate to not have to put Clyde in day care. Jeremy goes into the office two days a week and stays with Clyde the rest of the week, and Holly is flexible with her family business. Clyde now attends Mother's Day Out twice a week for socialization. He is doing so well,

James Family on the Disney Cruise

his teachers say that he is actually the class helper! He very much loves superheroes and comic books, he loves playing outside and swimming, and loves spending time at Mim and Papi's house (Holly's parents).

We have always had a heart for bringing children into our family through adoption but thought that was something we would do later in life. However, when we decided to expand our family, God lead us on this path. We really want to share the love and blessings we have with a child who doesn't have that and needs unconditional love. As much as we would love to bring a sibling set into our family, we feel that we are better equipped to take in one child at a time to ensure their success in adjusting and growing. We are open to taking possible future siblings to keep their bloodline together.

We would like to have a boy Clyde's age or younger to allow him to play a vital "big brother" role in welcoming a new child into our family! He is wonderful with other children, loves to share, and prays for his new brother every night! We have no racial preferences for a child. Our church is diverse and has many children who have been adopted - so they will feel very comfortable in our environment. We know that Clyde is very advanced verbally and do not expect that out of all of our children. We are okay with minor learning disabilities such as ADHD or dyslexia but no significant physical or medical conditions.

We could not be more excited to extend our family and to meet our son!

- **James Family**
  Jeremy, Holly & Clyde

The second item you can start working on while you wait for your license is your family book. No matter what avenue of adoption you pursue, everyone needs a family profile book.

This book about your family expands on the Dear Case Manager letter and gives a glimpse into your life in much more detail. Think of it as a Facebook or Instagram profile for your family. You want the book to be genuine, detailed, and professional. You can of course add artistic touches (you want it to reflect you!), but you don't want it to look like those first generation PowerPoint presentations with Clip Art and stick figures.

You want to include great photos, great captions, and showcase your great story. You want to highlight your immediate family, extended family, community, friends, house, and extracurricular activities. This book is where you want to shine.

Again, this project just spoke to my creative, marketing heart, and it was something I gladly took upon myself. If you do not want to design your own book, you can definitely hire someone to do this for you. Your agency may be a great resource for this. You can also contact me from my website HollyNicoleJames.com/FamilyProfileBook, and I offer a service to help with this, as well. We chose to tell our story through our "James Family Top 10 Photos":

1.   Our Engagement

2.   Our Wedding Day

In each section, we weaved in stories about our relationship, our desire to grow our family, and Clyde, his likes and interests and how we were already raising him. We wrote about our house, how we were set up to add more children, and how we foster creativity, free play, and family time. We covered our time spent in the great outdoors at my family's ranch, our family traditions on both sides, taking trips together and making memories, and how we like to vacation and have a crazy love for Disney.

And then, I wanted to showcase our support system. We wrote about our friends and family just waiting to embrace our little family and support us. We talked about how we have (and continue to add) diversity in our circle, ready to embrace any nationality of a child we may have. And we told about how we work to foster a loving, Christian home with fun, exploration, and a lot of social life.

This book was one of my favorite things to design and create. Don't forget, you want to ask for a lot of feedback from social work professionals to make sure you are including everything you need and putting your best foot forward. This book truly can be the difference between getting matched with a child or not. No pressure (*wink wink*). So to help you with a starting point, I wanted to share our book with you!

NUMBER 1

Our Engagement - We were friends for 2 years when we worked on the school newspaper together at Hanover Square University and then dated for a year and half when we got engaged! The best decision we ever made!

HELLO LIFE.

number 2

Our Wedding - April 24, 2008 at Sapienza Church. This was one of the best days of our life. We had 60 people in our bridal party and over 500 people in attendance celebrating our love and our new life together!

I now pronounce you Mr. & Mrs. Jerreau

THINGS THAT SMILE.

NUMBER 3

LOVED THIS.

LIFE is GOOD.

The Pregnancy - First comes love, then comes marriage then comes Clyde?! We could not have been more thrilled to add the first baby to our family - and a boy! Clyde was named after Jeremy's grandfather Clyde James.

142

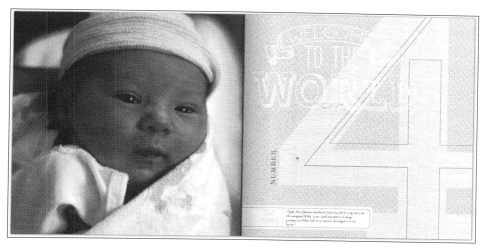

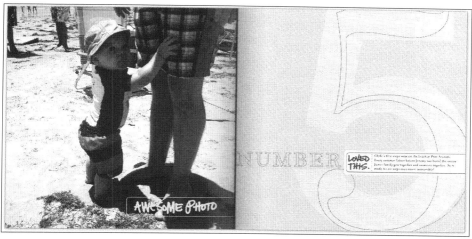

NUMBER

LIFE is GOOD.

HOME IS WHERE THE HUGS ARE

number 8

THE STORY

December 2012

LIFE in PICTURES

THIS PHOTO IS MY HEART

NUMBER

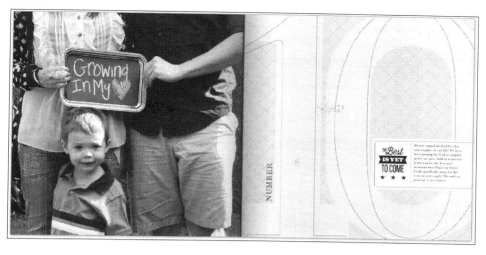

Growing In My ♥

NUMBER 10

THE Best IS YET TO COME ★★★

We are beyond thrilled for this next chapter in our life! We have been praying for God to prepare and/or save our next child to enter our home and for the love and roommates we will give to them! Clyde specifically prays for his bedroom mate nightly! He really is growing in our hearts!

FAMILY FRIENDS

LIFE is GOOD.

We are blessed with many friends in near an and unique life is on!

1) This is our friend Lucia and her son Harley. Holly & Lucia have been friends since high school youth group. She is a professional photographer and took all of our professional photos! 2) This is our friends Larissa, her husband Chris & daughter Clarisse. Holly & Larissa have been friends since high school & are our children are friends! 3) This is our friend Kelsey & her family. Holly & Kelsey have been friends since high school. 4) This is our friends Tara and Ty. Holly & Tara were roommates in college. 5) Jude adores these and all of these puppies! 6) There are all of Jude's friends celebrating him at his 1st birthday party! 7) This is our friends Ryan & Stephen, Jessica and Ryan have been friends since college. Ryan & Clyde share the same birthday! 8) These are our friends Ash, her daughter Vera & Charish. Holly worked with Ash & Charish on Student Programming board in college & have been friends ever since! 6) These are our friends the Dobbins family. They live next door, so Holly's parents and are Clyde's best.

aWEsome FAMILY

In addition to the awesome friends we have, we have a large extended family on high sides!

1) This is Holly's grandfather and her mom's side. He nattend 86 years old this year on the 4th of July! All Americans in person! 2) This is Holly's parents and sister on our Disney cruise! We live about 10 miles apart and spend a lot of time with them. 3) This is Jeremy's mom and sisters at her base! Mom is very loved! 4) This is Jeremy's mother and sister-in-law and two daughters celebrating Thanksgiving with us! 5) This is Holly's LARGE extended family. Every year after Christmas we have a progressive dinner at all of our houses. This is the gang that year! 6) This is Holly with her dad and his mom - a generations together right here! She will turn 84 this year! 7) This is Jeremy's dad, wife & kids of the family! We were all dressed up for a early Christmas picture on Christmas! 8) This is Holly's grandmother on her mom's side. She is my little Cajun grandma and will be 82 this year!

145

146

Notes

PART FOUR

Navigating CPS and the Legal System

66 Hopefully this broad overview of how CPS works, from an insider's perspective, will equip you and ease your fears to help you feel more prepared.

Chapter 13:

A Bunch of Legal Jargon and Being a Foster Parent

Just to forewarn you, this is the "meatiest" chapter in the whole book—mainly because there are so many legal terms and processes I want to familiarize you with in the CPS process and system. I also felt like we were least prepared for the legal side of CPS and parental rights during our adoption.

Our agency taught us why reunification of the child and their birth family was important, how they try to work with the birth families to make this a possibility, and about the child's potential emotional issues tied to reunification. They also went over some of the technical/paperwork responsibilities and checklists of what foster parents have to do on a monthly basis to complete reports for CPS. But beyond the paperwork requirements, our agency really did not cover any details of what the legal process of reunification looks like from a foster parent's perspective, other than you may have a few family visits or court appointments for their termination hearing. Maybe they did go into more detail. Maybe I just didn't understand a lot of the legal jargon and probably didn't want to process the reality of the process. At the time, during the training portion, I was still just worried about the matching process, managing trauma, and being a foster parent in general.

Hopefully this broad overview of how CPS works, from an insider's perspective, will equip you with definitions of common terminology and legal timelines to ease your fears and help you feel more prepared during the process.

I have to say, I was so scared to get involved with CPS and be assigned a CPS case manager. As a parent, just the letters "C.P.S." strike fear in you. It's sort of like when you see a police car on the freeway, even when you are going the speed limit. It strikes this deep-seated fear in your heart, making you feel like a hardened criminal trying to make it past GO. That's how I feel when I think of CPS entering my home and my life, scrutinizing my every move as a parent.

After going through the process of domestic adoption through CPS ourselves, our eyes and our hearts were opened to so many truths about the foster care and adoption process in the U.S.

The first thing you need to know before adopting through CPS is how the agency works, including the one-year reunification process that is put in place for the birth families when a child enters protective custody.

Removal and Foster Care

In every disruption in a home, meaning a child is removed from their home of origin, CPS must provide evidence that the child's environment is "either of an immediate danger to the physical health or safety of the child, or that the child has been a victim of neglect or sexual abuse."[14]

Once the child is in the care of CPS, the court will decide within 14 days if CPS will be the temporary conservators of the child or if the child will return to their home.

At this point, if CPS determines that the child does need to be under CPS' conservatorship, the agency attorney will seek necessary court orders for parental visitation, child support, paternity tests, psychology evaluations, drug assessments, etc.

The child will then be placed in a foster home, and a service plan will be put into place for the birth family with the goal being reunification of the child and parents. It is good to note that CPS' main goal is ALWAYS to reunify the original family unit.

Service Plan Timeline

A one-year service plan is issued to the birth parents at this point in the process. The timeline looks like this:

- Status Hearing: Occurs 60 days after the service plan has

14 DFPS.state.tx.us/Child_Protection/Investigations/parents_guide_to_investigation. asp

been issued

- First Permanency Hearing: Occurs 180 days after status hearing
- Second Permanency Hearing: Occurs 120 days after first permanency hearing
- Final Hearing: Occurs 120 days after second permanency hearing. CPS will either seek to terminate parental rights at this juncture or will drop the lawsuit and reunify the family.[15]

During this time, the biological family must complete certain tasks on their family action plan before reunification can be reconsidered. Required actions include things such as regular alcohol and drug testing, scheduled and monitored visits with their children, therapy, parenting education, domestic violence services, mental health evaluations, etc.

Usually around the six month mark, CPS will make a determination for the child's permanency based on how much of the family's action plan has been completed. CPS will then decide if their goal is still reunification or if, at this time, they will change the goal to permanency with a family member/non-family member. If there are no relatives found to be suitable caretakers, then they will look for a non-family member. This is when they

---

15 DFPS.state.tx.us/handbooks/CPS/Files/CPS_px_5400.asp

begin looking for foster-to-adopt families.

Legal Risk Placements

Next comes the legal risk broadcast. Once the child's goal has legally been changed to unrelated adoption through CPS, a legal risk broadcast is sent out to all agencies in the area, letting them know to submit foster-to-adopt families who would like to be considered as the child's family. This means that the agency intends to file a petition with family court to terminate parental rights. Note: the biological parents' rights have not been terminated at this point.

Since, in most cases, the child's foster parents are given first preference for adoption, legal-risk placements involve only those children whose current foster parents do not plan to adopt them. While these placements still involve the risk that the child may not become legally available for adoption, risk is substantially reduced once the agency has set the goal of "adoption" and has started the legal process to terminate parental rights.

That is why they put "risk" right there in the title. That is also why we were considered foster-to-adopt parents, not just adoptive parents. We were technically just foster parents with no guarantee of adoption until parental rights were terminated, and the adoption was finalized. While the majority of children in these circumstances eventually become available for adoption, there are just still no guarantees.

Foster-to-Adopt Family Chosen by a RAS Committee

Once CPS receives all the home studies from potential adoptive families, the child's CPS case manager and supervisor review the files and choose their top three. Those three families' agency case managers then go in front a board of people, which is called a RAS (Review Approval Screening) meeting.

Once you are chosen by the RAS committee, your agency will contact you notifying you that you will be foster parents and will let you know the schedule and plans for placing the child in your home.

Every situation is different, but the goal for introducing a new child to your home is to start with an initial day time visit or two, then have an overnight visit, followed by a weekend visit, and then transferring to full-time to your home. This is to make sure that the transfer is comfortable and that you can get to know each other before a more permanent placement.

This is, however, the perfect scenario and is not always feasible. Many times, as it was in our case, we just had one weekend visit, and then Nathaniel was permanently in our home two weeks later.

Being a Foster Parent

You did it.

> You survived the waiting period.

> You made it through the RAS committee and have been matched.

> That's it right?

> Not with foster-to-adopt through CPS. You now have two to three case managers who will be checking in with you a minimum of every 30 days:

> 1) CPS case manager

> 2) Agency case manager

> 3) Possible CASA case manager

> 4) Your child is also appointed a lawyer by the State to represent them. They may ask to meet with you as well. Ours never did but it can go either way.

Here are the biggest things that I learned during this part of the process of our adoption through CPS.

> All CPS case managers have unique supervisors who all have different goals and management processes. Every branch of CPS is

156

different. Even every county is different. Helpful, right?

However, here are some requirements that are going to be standard, legal routines you'll have to complete:

- A weekly activity log
- A monthly report
- Medication log
- Reports of any doctor, ER visits, etc. (even routine doctor and dentist visits are required.)
- Monthly visits from your CPS case manager (If you assigned a new manager and/or supervisor, you may have more than that in one-month.)

Here are some other important things to note:

- The average time social workers spend working at an agency is 18 months, so there is a possibility you may have multiple case managers. You also have one case manager for the foster stage, and then you are assigned another case manager during the adoption process.

- Depending on where you are in your process, you may also

be required to have biological sibling visits, court dates for biological parent updates, and parental rights termination court visits. You may also be called into the CPS office for planning meetings to discuss their progress and game plan before attending these court meetings.

• Parts of this process seem very tedious and cumbersome, but you have to understand that each case manager has 28 to 30 cases, potentially with multiple kids in each case. These logs and visits are a way for the case managers and supervisors alike to keep up with the children. They also provide legal documentation that is used in court and family determinations. And as much of a pain as it was sometimes, these records were also helpful for us personally when Nathaniel had medical problems and had to get tubes in his ears. We easily pulled out his file to see how many times he had been to the doctor for ear infections. It almost made me want to keep those kinds of records for Clyde as well. Almost.

• Always keep in the back of your mind that CPS is still the conservator of your child until they are adopted. You want them to be your cheerleader as well. You want them to like you and to root for you, so be mindful of that.

• Remember that you are doing this now for your child. It is a temporary assignment, and you will not always have this involvement in your life. I honestly had no intentions of ever adopting through CPS. I thought it was too messy. Too hard. Too unknown. After going through the process, I still feel that way. 100 percent. But I would totally do it all over again knowing that all adoptions, all pregnancies, and all life experiences can be messy, hard, and unknown.

These were all things I had no idea I was signing up for. I glossed over the realities thinking I was a foster-to-adopt mom, emphasis on the "adopt." I could never have foreseen I would be a foster mom for 342 days. It's a little ironic that I was least prepared to be a foster mom when that was a big bulk of my job.

And, of course, when you are going through the first mandatory classes, they mention court, surprise case manager home visits, and family visitation could be your reality. I kind of always thought in the back of my head that wouldn't be mine! But make sure you are still as prepared as possible and that you can actually go to these court dates and meetings.

But really, nothing can 100 percent prepare you for court and planning meetings with CPS until you experience it.

We were so very fortunate and did not have a bad experience with CPS. We did experience some of the typical things like multiple case managers, delayed response, and occasional lack of knowledge of our case. But we also found that, despite these frustrations, our case managers did have our son's best interest in mind, and our family would not be what it is today without these people. Our longest-running CPS case manager had over 30 cases at one point in our process, and our agency case manager had almost 60!

Can you even imagine having 60 cases at one time? Of those cases there could be multiple children in each case in different homes. And each one of these homes must be checked in on every 30 days. I cannot even imagine the pressure that was felt and the amount of hours that had to be put in to make this happen.

So while I understood and was compassionate, this also meant that it took a lot of attention to detail and patience on our part. This stage of our process felt so chaotic at times. We were trying to learn this new little person. He was trying to learn us. And then we had the weight of this process on us.

Ironically though, some of my sweetest memories as a mother came from this time being a foster momma. Watching Nate and Clyde's bond as brothers grow was something to behold. Nate arrived when he was eight months old, and the first few weeks, he would have to have his bottle in bed with Clyde before he would go to sleep. Otherwise, he would just cry and cry. Every night.

Clyde immediately became this protective big brother, telling everyone proudly that Nate was his adopted brother like a badge of honor. Nate's first word was actually "brother."

There is nothing like those first couple of months when we were getting to know each other. That first trusting laugh Nate gave us. The first time he called me momma. It's those sweet, tender, family growing moments, in the midst of all the chaos, that made the paperwork, the monthly visits, the court dates so much easier to endure.

I love the book of James. In fact, I would say it is one of my favorites books in the New Testament, as I really tend to stick to the Old Testament (I know I am totally weird and one of the few who picks the Old Testament over the New Testament). The book of James was written by, you guessed it, James, who was thought to be Jesus' half brother. He is writing to the church, to new Christians, after Jesus' death and resurrection, encouraging and commanding them to live a life of holiness. So many sermons you have heard in church—about loving your neighbor, faith without works, not judging others, controlling your tongue, all come from this short little five chapter book. So much wisdom is packed in here!

The verses I think are so encouraging during the adoption process come from James chapter 1, verses 2-7: "Consider it pure joy, my brothers and sisters, whenever you face trials of many kinds, because you know that the testing of your faith produces perseverance. Let perseverance finish its work so that you may be mature and complete, not lacking anything. If any of you lacks wisdom, you should ask God, who gives generously to all without finding fault, and it will be given to you. But when you ask, you must believe and not doubt, because the one who doubts is like a wave of the sea, blown and tossed by the wind. That person should not expect to receive anything from the Lord."

So James is saying, don't worry about trials you may go through—and I think many parts of the adoption process were trials for us. But the

Word says that produces faith and perseverance!

I also really think that this time of trials and testing, anxiety of the unknown, showed us God's hand so clearly. And more than that, I think it also prepared us for trials down the road where we could look back and say to ourselves thatGod already proved Himself and how much He loves us. He must be up to something.

If you ask God for wisdom, and he calls this into your life—if He calls adoption for your family— then do no doubt that! Because then you are just being tossed around like a wave of the sea. Be confident in God that He has called this into your life and that God, and only God, is in control every step of the way.

James 1:2-7

"Consider it pure *joy*, my brothers and sisters, whenever you face trials of many kinds, because you know that the testing of your *faith* produces perseverance. Let perseverance finish its work so that you may be mature and *complete*, not lacking anything."

Chapter 14:
What is a CASA worker?

CASA stands for Court Appointed Special Advocates for children. These are court appointed volunteers who are assigned to your children. They will also have monthly visits to your home, but their top interest during those is the child.

You see, as you go down this path, you may find that our system is broken and flawed. It is overflowing with children, and CPS and the State can't keep up with all of the needs and demands. Also, CPS' first goal is always reunification with the child's biological family. Well, that is not always in the best interest of the child. But the courts would have no other option but to take their advice. This is where child advocates come in.

There are nearly 1,000 CASA programs in 49 states, but this is a volunteer program so there are just not always enough! We were so fortunate that in our county, a CASA worker was required for each and every child who came through the system.

If you start to peel away and take a look at the requirements to be a CASA volunteer, it's quite extraordinary that they have so many people willing to step up to the occasion. While you don't have to be a social worker, lawyer, or anything like that, the commitment is quite extensive.

You have to pass a background check, participate in 30 hours of pre-volunteer training, and you have to be able to commit to staying with the case you sign up for in its entirety. This could be upwards of a year and half, and they estimate that you will devote about ten hours a week.

So why? Why would these people devote their time to this?

Because independent research has shown that children with a CASA volunteer are less likely to spend time in long-term foster care and less likely to reenter care.[16]

In fact, our CASA worker was one of the best parts of our experience. She truly loved Nathaniel and had his best interest at heart. It shined through every interaction she had with us. She had been with him since he came into CPS care (he was in a foster home from six weeks old until he came into our home at eight months old). And not only that, she grew to love our biological son and us as well. Not only did she know everything about Nate's case, she was so over-the-top thoughtful and brought Christmas presents, a birthday cake for Nathaniel's birthday, and gifts for National Foster Parent Day. And you better believe she came to every court date.

When we moved from foster placement to an adoption placement and she was no longer "assigned" to our family, she still checked in on us, and we still sent pictures. She even came to Nathaniel's court date to

16 Cynthia A. Calkins, M.S., and Murray Millar, Ph.D., "*The Effectiveness of Court Appointed Special Advocates to Assist in Permanency Planning,*" Child and Adolescent Social Work Journal, volume 16, number 1, February 1999

finalize his adoption as well as his party to celebrate officially becoming a James. She is truly a part of our family. We still text often, she comes to birthday parties, and we share in the same passions for helping children finding their forever homes.

These people have no ulterior motive except for the simple fact that they want to help children be in a safe and good environment. Here are some staggering statistics about how CASA and foster care work together, according to CASAForChildren.org:

- Over 600,000+ children pass through the U.S. foster care and family court systems annually
- The average child will spend nearly two years (20 months) in foster care
- On average each one of those children will change homes three time
- One year of CASA advocacy costs less than one month of foster care
- One staff member (as there is a paid supervisor) supports 30 volunteers who serve 75 children (Amazing!)

And what is crazy is that Nathaniel fell exactly into these statistics: He was in CPS care for almost 19 months, and he was in more than three homes during that time.

We owe so much of our adoption to CASA.

I specifically remember one of our court dates before parental rights were terminated, when had to go before the judge. Prior to this we had a huge meeting at the CPS building with everyone involved in the case (our CPS worker, our CASA worker, and our agency case manager), discussing the case so far and what to present in court. This is called a Family Group Decision Making Meeting.

/noun/ **fam·i·ly group de·ci·sion mak·ing meeting**

fam(ə)lē grōop də'siZHən mākiNG mēdiNG:

This meeting is supposed to get together the child's biological family, foster family, and all of the various case managers involved together in one room to discuss what the next and best course of action for the child should be.

However, we had no idea what this meeting was or that there was even a possibility of us attending any meetings at CPS' office. We just received a letter in the mail from CPS saying that we had to be there in five days to attend a meeting about Nathaniel, and if we could not be there physically, we needed to call in. We were stunned. We had just had all of our regular monthly visits from our agency, CPS, and CASA worker, and no one had referenced this meeting to us. Not to mention, we literally had no idea what this meeting was about.

We had just been assigned a new case manager at our adoption agency, a different person than our long-term manager we had from the beginning. Our location was growing, and they needed additional case managers to handle the large load of cases.

Our new case manager assured us that this was no big deal. They were just going to discuss the strategy for Nathaniel's upcoming court date. To this point we had not been to any court dates, so we did not know how that would go either. Our case manager told us to just bring some of our updates on Nate and maybe bring a few pictures of him with us to show everybody.

Okay, so no pressure, right?

We had Nathaniel in our home for about 45 to 60 days at this point, and the meeting was taking place right before Christmas. We have a tradition of taking family Christmas pictures every year, and I make Christmas cards to mail out to friends and family. This year was particularly special because we had Nate in our home for his first Christmas, and it was our first Christmas as a family of four. That particular year we got some amazing pictures, still some of my favorite, of a Texas Christmas on the beach. They were so cute, and I was so, so proud of my little family. So I thought those would be perfect to bring! He looked like such a little doll, and the photos showed just how much we all adored him. These were perfect to bring to the head of CPS!

So we get to the CPS building downtown, where we had never been before, and we are taken up to this little conference room, 10 by 10 at best, where we were set to have this big meeting. We were one of the first ones there except for a couple of the CPS supervisors whom we had never met. They were just casually talking to us and asking us about Nathaniel. They asked if we had brought his birth mom any pictures of Nathaniel.

Jeremy and I both looked at each other with eyes as large as silver dollars. What our agency case manager had failed to tell us, and probably assumed that we knew, was that this meeting was also supposed to include the birth family, whom we had never ever met. We did not have scheduled visitation, so we previously had no contact with any of Nathaniel's biological family.

We were stunned. And unprepared physically and emotionally.

At these meetings and at any court dates, you and your case managers are not supposed to give the birth family any of your personal information, details like your last name. Well our Christmas cards, which is what we brought to show off our pictures, had "James Family" written all over them and pictures of all four of us. In the end, these were not what we were supposed to bring, no matter how professional, cute, and proud of them I was. We were fortunate, in a way, that Nate's birth mom did not attend that day.

Aside from that little hiccup, the rest of the meeting went smoothly, something like this:

We discussed Nathaniel's placement and the history of his case. Based on the evidence presented that day, as well as information from previous history, all parties were in agreement that they would move to change his plan from reunification to unrelated adoption, and that there was a large possibility that termination of parental rights could come much earlier than the end of the standard year for the action plan. It could even possibly happen before Christmas, they said.

Then the court date came, and our assigned CPS case manager, the person who had met at our house every month and knew Nathaniel and his case intimately, could not attend because of a conflicting schedule. So our CPS supervisor, who we had never personally met in the few months Nathanial had been in our home, represented him in court that day. Because she was not involved in his case on a day-to-day basis, the supervisor had a lot of misinformation (including how old he was) while presenting information to the judge. In fact, the supervisor didn't really mention any of the items that we had met on the week before during the family group decision making meeting, as she was not in attendance of that meeting and suggested that reunification should still be on the table for the time being.

We were floored!

But then came in our CASA worker and supervisor. They had been prepared. They had all their information lined up in a row and spoke eloquently, calmly, and matter of fact. Not only that, they had found legal information very relevant to our case that CPS had no idea about, just by doing some simple research.

Our termination hearing did not come as early as we thought it might after the planning meeting. We also had received some extra requirements to satisfy the biological family plans that we felt were extreme, given the actual situation. However, it could have been so much worse if not for the information that our CASA team provided.

As I said earlier, some of this is due to CPS' overwhelming responsibilities. Some of this was just plain bad timing. And some was due to our lack of knowledge on the process. We were so thankful to have our CASA worker presenting the situation to the court in a much more realistic way.

Many times, the court will take the suggestion of the CASA volunteer with equal weight as CPS' recommendation. You want to very much befriend your CASA worker (and hopefully as in our case you won't even have to try to do that!). They will go to bat for you when needed.

If your area does NOT have a CASA worker or program, you can contact CASA directly to see about setting up a program. Hopefully, your agency can help you with this, as well.

Chapter 15:
HELP! I Really Need Somebody!

Y ou never want to think about things going wrong or problems arising, but what if they do? Who can you turn to?

We were so fortunate that we did not hit any major bumps in the road, but there were definitely some snags. Things happened that we did not completely agree with. And sometimes we found it hard, as you might, too, to parent a child and fight for their best interest, when you are not legally their parent and are still answering to other entities.

First of all, I suggest working with an adoption lawyer early on. Our agency said we did not need to do this until the end of the process Yes, you do not technically need to, and hiring a lawyer can become costly. (Remember: You also have adoption tax refunds at the end of the year that will cover a lot of these costs.) But I wish we would have done this sooner so we could have a lawyer's perspective and advice and even a lawyer's voice in the middle of conflict, even though our issues were minor.

Also, going back to how important an agency is, they can and will do a lot of navigating difficulties for you, as well. If you are having scheduling issues or questions about the process, they can help direct you in the way that you should go based on their knowledge and experience. They should always be your first line of defense. Your agency would also be a great resource for adoption lawyer references. They should have a list of lawyers that they have worked with in the area.

We did have an instance, I would say about half way through the process, where our CPS case manager failed to schedule an extra visit with us that month and only had two days left in the month to make the visit to meet her deadlines. The case manager called me on a Wednesday evening at 5:30 p.m. She called and said that she had to schedule an extra visit and could come on Friday, less than 48 hours from this phone call. Both my husband and I work, but my husband worked, at the time, only on Tuesdays, Thursdays, and Sundays. So we were always able to accommodate visits, never missed or canceled one, and never had any problems.

This particular week, however, was a unique week. I work with my dad who owns a small business. Small meaning there are five people running three different businesses. My dad, my mom, my sister, and my uncle (who is also one of the five people working for these businesses) had gone out of town, and I was left running different parts of these businesses.

My family is also my backup child care, and this happened to fall on the same weekend my husband had to go to a conference for work.

So it was just me, my children, and me running three businesses while everyone was gone. And on top of all of that, our agency had already scheduled a visit with us for that Friday. As you can imagine, this was already a little bit of a stressful week for me. So I explained the situation and politely asked that we reschedule for Monday when everyone would be back in town.

She said no. Flat out no. She said she had to have this visit, per her supervisor, and she could just come and pick up Nathaniel if she had to in order to make this visit happen.

Um. Yeah no. I was not about to have basically a stranger come and pick up my 13-month-old son and just take him somewhere. No, no, no.

So I called my agency case manager in a panic asking what to do—or if there was anything I even could do?! He explained that as conservator of Nathaniel, CPS technically COULD come get him at any time, even though they should not. So I should be accommodating and let them have the visit. This being my first time through the process, I shrugged my shoulders, rearranged my already hectic week, and they did their visit as demanded.

If I had to do that today, knowing what I know now, I would have also contacted my CASA worker right away, and then potentially my lawyer (who I didn't have at the time because we were waiting for closer to the consummation process as suggested). I wouldn't have contacted my lawyer for any legal action, but more as a counsel for what I could do within my legal rights and as an added layer of confidence to my decision-making. Who knows, should I have contacted my CASA worker and my lawyer, they may have given me the exact same advice my agency worker gave me.

Please do not let me give you the idea that you do not want to be accommodating and cooperative. You absolutely want your case managers to like you, and you want a smooth process. But you are the parent, and you have to protect your children, no matter what that looks like.

If you have more serious conflict, there are many CPS reform organizations in each state that you can turn to, as well. StrengtheningFamilies.org is a great place to start. I only suggest going this route if there are major issues with your case, such as a disruption or removal from your home. My story above probably doesn't necessitate getting a million people involved and really making your case manager mad. Remember, this reflects badly on them and jeopardizes their job. So keep that in mind when determining how far you need to go, as well.

But if you do need to take these measures, you will obviously want to lean on your adoption agency, your lawyer, and your CASA advocate to point you in the direction of what legal recourse needs to be taken.

I also do not want to paint an awful picture of CPS. Our experience was overall very positive. We could tell that our case manager had a tremendous caseload, but she still had Nathaniel's best interest in mind and wanted his forever home to be with us. For that, I am forever grateful.

You also want to use your entire network. Lean on your adoptive friends. You will be surprised how many people they know and can refer you to locally. And at the very least, they can lend you support, prayers, and encouragement. You have no idea how much you will need this, in the big and small areas.

But the biggest person you need to go to with any worries first and foremost is God. I know I have already said this, so I hope I am not beating a dead horse here. But I truly do not know how we would have made it through the process without the peace and comfort of knowing that God was in control.

In the book of Joshua, Joshua is leading the Israelites into the Promised Land, and Moses, their leader, has died. The Israelites have been wandering in the desert for 40 years after decades of slavery in Egypt. So the people are scared and worried that they won't make it to the "Promised Land" or if they do, what will be waiting for them? And I am sure Joshua was not so confident himself. He had some large shoes to fill and thousands of people depending on him! And God tells Joshua in chapter 1 verses 2 to 6:

"Moses my servant is dead. Now then, you and all these people, get ready to cross the Jordan River into the land I am about to give to them—to the Israelites. I will give you every place where you set your foot, as I promised Moses. Your territory will extend from the desert to Lebanon, and from the great river, the Euphrates—all the Hittite country—to the Mediterranean Sea in the west. No one will be able to stand against you all the days of your life. As I was with Moses, so I will be with you; I will never leave you nor forsake you. Be strong and courageous, because you will lead these people to inherit the land I swore to their ancestors to give them."

Wow! Our God knows our fears. And he reiterates His promises to us. He will never leave us or forsake us! And then God says, in verse 9: "Have I not commanded you? Be strong and courageous. Do not be afraid; do not be discouraged, for the Lord your God will be with you wherever you go."

So not only does He encourage us, He then commands us to be strong and courageous. That is very different than just telling us we should or could do something—God commanded us to be bold!

He has appointed you as a guardian to a little child or children waiting for you to be their forever parent. To fight for them. Cry for them. Pray for them. Go to bat for them. And there will be many nights where you think, how can I even do this? I am just one person. Fortunately for us, we don't have to be everything. We just have to do what God commands of us, and He takes care of the rest.

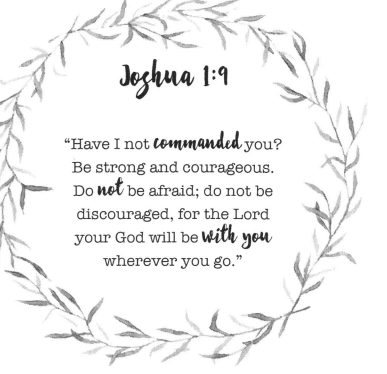

Joshua 1:9

"Have I not **commanded** you? Be strong and courageous. Do **not** be afraid; do not be discouraged, for the Lord your God will be **with you** wherever you go."

Notes

PART **FIVE**

While You Wait and Resources

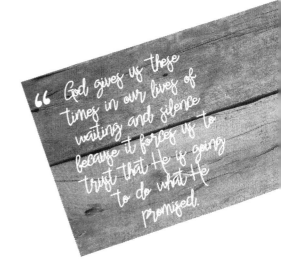

" God gives us these times in our lives of waiting and silence because it forces us to trust that He is going to do what He promised.

Chapter 16:
Adoption Adventure Tools

I think that God gives us these times in our lives of waiting and silence because it forces us to trust that He is going to do what He promised. And when He finally does what it is that He set out to do, we can see clearly that it was God who gave us these blessings and that He is faithful to us no matter what.

Look at Abraham and Sarah. They waited how long for a child? Abraham was 100 years old when his son was born! Now, they aren't the perfect picture of patience, but there is something comforting about that, too, isn't there?

So I encourage you during this time—whether you are just starting to think about adoption or you are starting the process right now—to do several things to fill the silence and use this time to your advantage.

• If you have not already, start preparing current children in your home for a new addition. We started our first adoption when Clyde, our oldest, was just two and a half. We talked about adoption with him from the minute we started the process. A lot of people thought he was too young or that we were setting him up for disappointment. But what we found was, 1) our talks normalized the adoption, and 2) he was SO excited and instead of feeling like he was giving up his place to make way for a sibling, he was eagerly anticipating our new family member.

• Start journaling everything now! I so wish I had done this. I am not saying you have to do this every day, but record the big things, the milestones. Your feelings and emotions are all so raw and fresh. And when it is all finalized, it is so amazing to go back and reflect on the experience. Journaling also helps you see exactly where God was working in the waiting and frustrations. A lot of times you won't have even realized it in the moment!

• Organize all of your paperwork in files. You will need these documents throughout the process and even afterwards. I don't care if you're a Type A personality or not. Paperwork is something you need to pay attention to, keep up with, and get good at.

• Spend time in the Word. Our agency provided us with a 30-day daily devotional called "Abba, Father." It was so great because it gave us so many ideas to think and pray through. It was encouraging and helped us to stay the course, even when we felt discouraged.

• Date your spouse! Your life is about to drastically change—for the better. You are about to have more work to do for your child than you ever thought possible. So take advantage of the down time now. You will be glad that you did!

• Prep your friends and family. If you are adopting internationally or through foster care, you are entering a totally different type of parenting. This is a good time to let your friends and family know how it could be different and what you may need from them. We have a very large, close family who love children and babies, and the first weekend we kept Nathaniel, he was eight months old. We had to prepare everyone that we did not know how he was going to react to being in a new place with new people. While we loved that everyone was so excited, we were not going to be accepting visitors that first weekend. Adopting through foster care is very different from bringing a baby home from the hospital. Our family was very understanding because we set their expectations ahead of time.

Adoption Resources

I also wanted to share some additional resources that were helpful for me during this process. There are a lot of resources out there! You can Google any number of parenting topics and almost always find what you need. But these were near and dear to my heart or personal recommendations from my adoptive momma friends:

Books

• *Adopt Without Debt: Creative Ways to Cover the Cost of Adoption*, by Julie Gumm: This is very helpful for navigating the overwhelming costs of infant and international adoption.

• *The Connected Child: Bring Hope and Healing to Your Adoptive Family*, by Dr. Karyn Purvis, David Cross, and Wendy Sunshine: This book comes highly, highly recommended in the adoption world. Pretty much any adoption resource section you find will mention this book that helps parents better connect with their foster and adoptive children. *The Connected Child* offers practical tools from a beautiful Christian perspective.

• *God Found Us You*, by Lisa Tawn Bergren: This is an absolutely beautiful children's book for adopted children. I cried my eyes out when I read this, but it gives such a great explanation and encouragement for the adopted child.

Websites

• Adopt.org: This is just an overall great resource that supports the adoption community. They have great information for learning about adoption, a place to connect adoptive parents, and a lot of great adoption causes to support.

• AdoptUSKids.org: Because state licensing requirements vary from state to state, this is a great place to check the requirements for your state. It is also an all-around great resource to learn more about the foster care system and adoption through foster care.

• CASAForChildren.org: CASA for Children provides everything you need to know about CASA services, how you can help and get involved, and information about children in the foster care system. Also, if you do not have CASA workers in your area, you can request services in your area through their website.

• ChildWelfare.gov: This is a great resource to learn about foster care and adoption in the United States. So many topics are covered here, and the site offers a variety of resources. This site will also give you a great start to researching your state requirements.

- DaveThomasFoundation.org: The Dave Thomas Foundation was founded by Wendy's founder and CEO. They are a 501(3)c that awards grants to adoptive families and increases awareness about foster care and adoption. They also provide a lot of free resources for professionals and adoptive parents alike.

- HollyNicoleJames.com: If you want to keep up with my thoughts on parenting and adoption, you can follow me on my blog. I discuss a variety of topics regarding adoption, share our story, and provide a lot of additional resources. I also offer services on designing family books and developing your Dear Case Manager letter.

- SensoryWorld.com: This company offers books, CDs, and loads of information on sensory disorders. This resource could come in handy down the road, and they even provide a list of 10 common signs of sensory processing disorder. My children personally do not have any sensory issues, but many of my friends' kiddos do. This has been helpful for me to even learn more to help parent alongside them!

- Strengthening-Families.org: This is a CPS reform organization that provides resources for families connecting them with groups across the U.S. who advocate for families. Their list of partner organizations is a great start for finding help in your state should any problems arise with CPS during your adoption.

• Travel.State.gov: This website offers a wealth of information on international adoption. Under U.S. law, there are two distinct intercountry adoption processes: the Hague Convention process and the non-Hague Convention process. This website can be a great guide to the legalities and answer your questions about both processes.

Conferences and Events

• Created for Care Retreat: This retreat encourages, equips, and connects foster and adoptive mothers. I have not personally attended the large retreat, and for the moment these large sessions have been put on hold, but I have been fortunate enough to attend a mini-retreat hosted by a friend who had attended and wanted to share with us adoptive mommas. I seriously cannot recommend events like this enough. Just being able to connect with other adoptive mommas is huge. You can still purchase past conference videos and resources from their website. I highly recommend watching those! Who knows, you may want to host your own mini retreat! Learn more at CreatedForCare.org.

• Wait No More Conference: The Wait No More Conference is hosted by Focus on the Family. The purpose of this event is to join together adoption agencies, church leaders, and ministry partners to raise awareness and recruit families for children waiting for permanent homes. After we were rejected from our first adoption agency, we attended this conference to learn more about adoption in our area and how to choose our agency. To see a schedule of host cities and conference dates, visit ICareAboutOrphans.org/whatwedo/waitnomore/

Services

• Adoption lawyers: Your agency can provide good recommendations for attorneys they have worked with in their area. However, if they do not have access to these resources, the American Academy of Adoption Lawyers is also a good place to start. The American Academy of Adoption Attorneys is a national association of approximately 340 attorneys who practice or have otherwise distinguished themselves in the field of adoption law. The Academy's work includes promoting the reform of adoption laws and disseminating information on ethical adoption practices. You can find a listing of attorneys in your area at AdoptionAttorneys.org.

• Christian Adoption Consultants: If you are looking to partner with an experienced consultant to help you navigate the world of adoption,

Christian Adoption Consultants is a great agency to work with for infant and international adoptions. They help with financial advice, education, and guidance. They work as your personal advocate and most of their staff are not only experienced consultants but most are adoptive parents themselves. To find out more about their services, visit ChristianAdoptionConsultants.com.

• IRS Adoption Credit: The IRS Adoption Credit is something you will need to familiarize yourself with. I suggest consulting a CPA to make sure all of your paperwork is correct. Here are some other sources that can be helpful to be informed about the changing laws:

- IRS: IRS.gov/taxtopics/tc607.html

- Fund Your Adoption: FundYourAdoption.tv/adoption-tax-credit/

- Creating a Family – The National Infertility & Adoption Education Nonprofit: CreatingaFamily.org/adoption-category/2017-adoption-tax-credit-announced/

Glossary

I also wanted to leave you with a handy list of terms defined throughout the book, as well as some terms I did not get a chance to touch on that you may come across. I know I gave you a lot of information that can be overwhelming. So if you want to reference these topics later, you will have a convenient guide.

• Adoption assistance/Special care subsidy (page 99): "State and federal programs that provide financial and medical assistance to help parents care for children with special needs after adoption is finalized." *(Source: Adopt.org/glossary)*

• Adoption placement paperwork (page 43): "Adoption placement is the meeting in which the child's case manager, the biological family's case manager, and the adoptive family sign paperwork officially placing the child in the home for adoption. The State will ask the adoptive family to read and sign paperwork and answer any questions the biological family may have." *(Source: TexasCASA.org/wp-content/uploads/2013/08/Adoption-Webinar_PPT.pdf)*

• Adoption services (page 43): The adoption branch of DFPS. In the foster-to-adopt process, you will have a case manager from the foster services branch, but once you start the adoption finalization process, you are transferred to the adoption services branch and will have a different case manager.

- Can I Parent This Child?/Children's needs questionnaire (pages 69, 79-80, 115): A detailed questionnaire that outlines the parameters of children you will be willing to take into your home. This will help your agency in the matching process and will also help you and your spouse discuss different possible scenarios. This questionnaire varies, but it includes medical history, social needs, special needs, physical characteristics, and race.

Children's Needs Questionnaire

General Questions

Adoption Parameters
Age of Child/Children
Gender
Number of Children
Religious Background
Languages Spoken
Race/Ethnicity

Birth Parent's Background
Information available on parents
Criminal Record
Alcoholism
Drug Abuse
Mental Illness
Mental Disabilities
Slow Learner
Prostitution

Child's Profile

Birth History
Child conceived from Incest
Child conceived from Sexual Assault
Premature Birth
Low Birth Rate
Genetic Risks
Prenatal Alcohol Exposure
Prenatal Drug Exposure
Fetal Alcohol Syndrome
Test Positive for Drug at Birth

Physical Disabilities
Limps
Leg Braces
Crutches
Hypertension
Wheelchair
Missing Limbs

Exhibiting Behaviors
Aggression   Stealing
Anxiety   Temper Tantrums
Hyperactivity   Withdrawal
Dependency   Sexual Behavior
Lying

Environment Exposure
Emotional Abuse
Physical Abuse
Sexual Abuse
Neglect
Multiple Caregivers
Abandonment

Medical Diagnosis
ADHD   Hearing Impaired
AIDS   HIV Positive
Allergies   Heart Defect
Anxiety Disorder Hepatitis B
Asperger's   Hepatitis C
Asthma   Mental Disability
Attachment Disorder Mood Disorder
Autism   Partial to full Deafness
Cerebral Palsy   Personality Disorder
Cleft Palate   Schizophrenia
Cross Eyed   Spina Bifida
Diabetes   Vision Impaired
Downs Syndrome
Eating Disorders
Epilepsy

• CASA worker (page 164): "CASA stands for Court Appointed Special Advocate for children. These are court appointed volunteers who are assigned to foster children. They will also have monthly visits to your home, but their top interest during those visits is the child. There are nearly 1,000 CASA programs in 49 states." *(Source: CASAforChildren.org)*

• Consummation (page 43): "This is a common term used in adoption world lingo. Consummation is the final court hearing in which the adoption is finalized with the court. At this hearing, conservatorship of the child is given to the adoptive parents, and the State's case is closed for that child." *(Source: TexasCASA.org/wp-content/uploads/2013/08/Adoption-Webinar_PPT.pdf)*

• CPS (page 111): "Stands for Child Protective Services. They are the investigative arm of DFPS (defined below) to determine if a child is experiencing neglect and/or abuse in their family. Caseworkers decide if there are any threats to the safety of all children in the home. If so, they determine if the parents are willing and able to adequately manage those threats to keep children safe. If CPS decides that children aren't safe, the caseworker starts protective services." *(Source: DFPS.state.tx.us/child_protection/investigations/)*

• Dear Case Manager letter (pages 137-138): The Dear Case Manager letter is a one-page letter written to introduce you and your family to the case manager of the child you are submitting your home study for in a CPS adoption. This letter is used by CPS to help determine three families who should advance to the RAS committee meeting.

• DFPS: Stands for Department of Family and Protective Services. DFPS encompasses the State's entire child and family department including CPS, kinship care, foster care, and adoption services.

• Domestic infant adoption (page 92): Domestic infant adoption involves the prospective adoptive family working with an agency to prepare a home study and portfolio for pregnant birth mothers to review as they choose an adoptive family for their child.

It is common for birth parents to want to get to know the adoptive family a little better. Today, most adoption professionals encourage an "open adoption" because it helps the birth mother feel more confident in the family she's chosen and for the life she has envisioned for her child.

• Domestic Waiting Child (page 98): Waiting children are children in the State's CPS program who are currently in foster homes. The court has terminated the parental rights of both birth parents and all appeals have been exhausted. This term is synonymous with "legally free" children for adoption.

These children are typically part of sibling sets and are often five years of age and older. Pursuing adoption of a domestic waiting child can be a faster route to adoption, and you also don't have to jump through all the hoops of being a foster parent.

However, with this program, you do not receive monthly reimbursement and subsidy advantages like you would with the foster-to-adopt child subsidy, unless they are eligible for the special needs subsidy. Again, this varies by state so definitely check with your agency.

As with children in the foster-to-adopt program, the agency typically does not charge anything to adopt waiting children. Usually your only costs associated with a waiting child adoption are minimal legal fees.

• Dossier (page 123): "A collection of papers containing very detailed information about you. The vast majority of countries open to international adoption require prospective adoptive parents to compile a dossier. Compiling a dossier involves gathering and notarizing documents and then adding various seals from your county, your state, and the U.S. government." *(Source: Adoption.com/dossier)*

• Family care plan (service plan) (page 152): This is a list of tasks that must be completed in a one-year time frame for a biological family to be considered to reunite with their children who are in DFPS care after abuse and/or neglect. The biological family must complete things such as regular alcohol and drug testing, scheduled and monitored visits with their children, therapy, parenting education, domestic violence services, mental health evaluations, etc.

• Family disruption (page 151): "Sometimes called failed placement, disruption occurs when a child leaves the adoptive home prior to the finalization of the adoption. This can occur in three situations: (1) In a legal risk adoption, usually involving a newborn infant, the birth parents revoke their consent to the adoption, during the time period when this is still possible; (2) The adoptive parents choose not to continue with their plan to parent the child for reasons of their own; or (3) The agency disrupts the adoption if the adoptive parents are not complying with post-placement requirements or are endangering the child in some way." *(Source: Adopt.org/glossary)*

• Family group decision making meeting (page 167): "A long meeting planned to empower and guide a team of social workers, family members, and/or foster parents or caretakers to make the best possible decisions regarding a child's future. In CPS situations, this commonly involves conversations about where the children will live and which adults will be responsible for raising them. However, sometimes it might involve discussions of the extended family continuing to be involved in the lives of the children without the children actually living with them." *(Source:HelpStartsHere.org/kids-and-families/family-safety/family-safety-your-options-are-you-a-grandparent-or-other-relative-with-a-child-in-protective-services-custody.html)*

• Family profile book (page 139): The family profile book is an extended version of the Dear Case Manager letter, expanded into a book about your family, to share with the RAS committee or birth mother when they are choosing a forever family. It gives a glimpse into your life that goes into much more detail than the letter. Think of it as a Facebook or Instagram profile for choosing you as a family. You want this to be genuine, detailed, and professional.

You can absolutely add artistic touches (you want it to reflect you!), but you don't want it to look like those first generation PowerPoint presentations with Clip Art and stick figures.

You are going to want great photos, great captions, and a great story. You want to show your immediate family, extended family, community, friends, house and extracurricular activities. This is where you want your family to shine. To see an example of our book, go to page 139.

• Family team meeting: "The family team meeting (FTM) is different from the family group decision making meeting. These gatherings are usually held before CPS files a court petition for removal, when children are still living at home with their biological parents. The family team meeting is a way for CPS to decide quickly if safety concerns can be addressed without having to remove the child. FTMs are voluntary and family, friends, and relatives will meet and come up with a plan for how to address the safety concerns." *(Source: ParentResourceGuide.texaschildrenscommission. gov/library_item/gov.texaschildrenscommissionparent_resource_guide/12)*

• Foster care: "A temporary arrangement in which adults provide for the care of a child or children whose birth parent is unable to care for them. Foster care is not where juvenile delinquents go. It is where children go when their parents cannot, for a variety of reasons, care for them.

Foster care can be informal or arranged through the courts or a social service agency. The goal for a child in the foster care system is usually reunification with the birth family, but may be changed to adoption when this in the child's best interest. While foster care is temporary, adoption is permanent." *(Source: Adopt.org/what-foster-care)*

• Foster care subsidy (page 99): DFPS provides assistance and financial reimbursement to foster families. Check with your state to determine the rate specific to your state's program.

• Foster-to-adopt (pages 94-95): "Child placement in which birth parents' rights have not yet been severed by the court or in which birth parents are appealing the court's decision but foster parents agree to adopt the child if/when parental rights are terminated. Social workers place the child with specially-trained foster-to-adopt parents who will work with the child during family reunification efforts but who will adopt the child if the child becomes available for adoption. The main reason for making such a placement is to spare the child another move." *(Source: Adoption.com/wiki/foster-adoption_(glossary))*

• Goal (page 32): "Each child in foster care is assigned a goal which may be reunification with the birth family, adoption, long-term foster care, or independent living. A court hearing is required for a goal to be changed. Usually a child must have a goal of adoption before adoptive families are considered." *(Source: Adopt.org/glossary)*

• Guardian ad litem: "A person, sometimes an attorney, appointed by the court to ensure that the child's best interests are addressed in court hearings and other proceedings. In many jurisdictions, court-appointed special advocate (CASA) volunteers serve as guardians ad litem." *(Source: DaveThomasFoundation.org/adoption-guide/terms/)*

• Hague Convention (page 101): "A multinational agreement designed to promote the uniformity and efficiency of international adoptions."

(Source: Family.FindLaw.com/adoption/glossary-of-adoption-terms.html)

• Home licensing (page 43): Many states require that families providing foster care must be licensed, certified, or approved; however, licensing rules and regulations vary from state to state. To learn about local rules and resources and find agencies in your area, go to AdoptUSKids.org/adoption-and-foster-care/how-to-adopt-and-foster/state-information.

• Home study (page 125): "A study of the prospective adoptive family and their home, life experiences, health, lifestyle, extended family, attitudes, support system, values, beliefs, and other factors relating to the prospective adoption. This information is summarized in an adoption study or home study report." *(Source: Family.FindLaw.com/adoption/ glossary-of-adoption-terms.html)*

• International adoption (page 100): The adoption process when trying to adopt from a country outside of your own. International adoption is similar to domestic adoption in that both are working towards the same legal goal of transferring parental rights to the adoptive parents. International adoption varies in the legal process and amount of paperwork that is required to make the adoption happen. The country from which you want to adopt may or may not be part of the Hague Convention.

International adoption usually costs anywhere between $25,000 to $40,000 depending on the country and your agency. Many of these fees are dictated by the international country and consist of legal fees and travel costs.

• Kinship adoption (page 132): "Kinship adoption is the adoption of a child by his or her relative, either biological or by marriage. Adoption of a child by a grandparent, aunt, uncle, or other member of the extended family is a kinship adoption." *(Source: Definitions.USLegal.com/k/kinship-adoption/)*

- Legal guardian (page 134): "A person who fulfills some of the responsibilities of a legal parent while the courts or birth parents may continue to hold other legal responsibilities for the child. Guardianship is subject to ongoing supervision by the court and ends by court order or when the child reaches the age of majority. Guardianship may be used as an alternative to adoption in some kinship care situations in which a child's relative is assuming a parental role but prefers not to adopt. In some states, such guardians are entitled to the same benefits as foster or adoptive parents." *(Source: Adopt.org/glossary)*

- Legal risk placement/adoption (page 154): "A legal risk placement is when a child is placed with a prospective adoptive family but the child is not yet legally free for adoption. A child becomes legally free once a parent's parental rights are terminated or the parents have relinquished their parental rights. In the case of a legal risk placement either the termination hasn't occurred yet or it has and is being contested in court by the birth family. When a family takes in a child who is considered to be a legal risk placement, that family must understand that the child could be placed back with his birth family. This is not just a legal risk in terms of the courts, but a risk of the prospective adoptive family's heart." *(Source: Adoption.com/wiki/legal_risk_adoptions)*

• Legal risk broadcast (pages 80-81): A profile put together on a child when DFPS is looking for families to place a child in a foster-to-adopt home. This report is sent out to all the local adoption agencies and includes information such as health, social, educational, and genetic history. Many times this information is gathered through the daily reports compiled from the foster family.

• Legally free children (page 31): "Since a child can have only one set of legal parents at a time, when the parental rights of a child's biological parents are legally terminated, either by their death, legal consent, or by a forced termination by the court, then the child becomes legally free, to be adopted by another set of legal parents." *(Source: Adoption.com/wiki/legally_free)*

• Match/matching process (page 79): "In adoption, matching is the process of finding prospective families for a child. A match may refer to a family that a child's worker has selected or is strongly considering, but it also may refer to a family that the family's worker or adoption exchange worker is merely suggesting to the child's worker." *(Source : Adopt.org/glossary)*

• Non-recurring adoption expenses (page 96): "The reasonable and necessary adoption fees, court costs, attorney fees, and other expenses that are directly related to the legal adoption of a child with special needs, which are not incurred in violation of State or Federal law, and which have not been reimbursed from other sources or funds.

Other allowable costs of the adoption incurred by or on behalf of the parents and for which parents carry the burden for payment, may include: the adoption home study, health and psychological examinations, supervision of the placement prior to the adoption, transportation and reasonable costs of lodging, and food for the child and/or the adoptive parents when necessary to complete the adoption process." *(Source: CalSWEC.Berkeley.edu/sites/default/files/uploads/seg15_ho72_aap8.pdf)*

• Non-related adoption/unrelated adoption (page 97): Adoption of a child is opened up to adoptive families once all avenues of relatives have been exhausted as possible permanent families for the child.

• Open adoption (pages 92, 94): "Also known as a cooperative adoption, this type of adoption allows for some form of association between the birth family, adoptees, and adoptive parents. This can range from picture and letter sharing to phone calls to contact through an intermediary to open contact between the parties themselves. Many adoptions of older children and teens are at least partially open, since the children may know identifying or contact information about members of their birth families or may want to stay in touch with siblings placed separately.

An open adoption agreement spells out the terms of the contact between the parties in an open adoption. An open adoption agreement can specify frequency and manner of contact between adoptive and birth families and/or between siblings placed separately." *(Source: Adopt. org/glossary)*

• PMC: "Stands for permanent managing conservatorship. The court can award this to CPS, family members, close friends, or foster parents without granting adoption. Only a court can legally decide this. Parents' rights are always affected when a court names someone other than the parent as the Permanent Managing Conservator of a child. However, the biggest effect comes from the court's decision whether or not to terminate their parental rights." *(Source: DFPS.state.tx.us/adoption_and_ foster_care/about_adoption/pmc.asp)*

• RAS meeting (pages 83, 155): Stands for review and approval staffing. This committee is made up of all of the child's case managers including CPS and CASA reps. These workers meet with the top three families' agency case managers to determine placement of the child. The agency case managers attend RAS on the family's behalf to present the family and their family profile book to the RAS team and advocate for family's selection.

• Redacted file (page 43): "In Texas adoption, you do not receive all of the child's health, social, education, and genetic history (HSEGH report) until finalization of the adoption. Before adoption finalizes, the prospective parents are given the opportunity to look through the file that includes:

    - The child's section

    - The family section

    - The sibling section, but only sibling medical information regarding siblings included in the same legal case

    - Legal and case narratives

    - Previous investigations, including any investigations conducted by Child Care Licensing in which the child to be adopted was an alleged or designated perpetrator or victim"

CPS does not give the prospective adoptive parents a copy of these records to keep until the adoption is consummated."

(Source: DFPS.state.tx.us/handbooks/CPS/Files/CPS_pg_6900.asp)

- Respite care (page 123): "Temporary care provided for a child in order to give the child's foster or adoptive parents time off or a rest from parenting." *(Source: Adopt.org/glossary)*

- Reunification (page 95): "Occurs when a child who has been in foster care returns to his or her birth family. Reunification is the goal for many children in foster care." *(Source: Adopt.org/glossary)*

- SAMA techniques (page 110): "Stands for Satori Alternatives to Managing Aggression. It is an integrated system in helping parents to prevent physical aggression, contain a person when they are a danger to themselves or to others, retrieve objects, and protect ones self from aggressive acts. This is part of the pre-service training, but this specific program may not be required by your agency or your agency may use a substitute program." *(Source: SAMATraining.com)*

- Service plan (family care plan) (page 152): A one-year service plan is issued to the birth parents once a child enters into protective services. The timeline looks like this:

  - Status hearing: 60 days after the service plan has been issued

  - 1st permanency hearing: 180 days after status hearing

  - 2nd permanency hearing: 120 days after 1st permanency

hearing

- Final hearing: 120 days after 2nd permanency hearing. CPS will either seek to terminate parental rights at this juncture or will drop the lawsuit and reunify the family.

During this time, the biological family must complete certain tasks on their family action plan before reunification can be reconsidered. They need to complete things such as regular alcohol and drug testing, scheduled and monitored visits with their children, therapy, parenting education, domestic violence services, mental health evaluations, etc.

• Social workers: "Help individuals, families, and groups restore or enhance their capacity for social functioning and work to create societal conditions that support communities in need.

When you have a foster child, they will have several social workers, a DFPS social worker, a CASA social worker, your adoption agency case manager, and possibly a court appointed attorney for the child called an attorney ad litem. Often referred to as case managers." *(Source: SocialWorkers.org)*

• Special needs (page 98): "In the context of adoption, under federal guidelines, children with special needs are children who have a condition or history making it difficult to place them without adoption assistance, and who cannot or should not be returned to their birth families. Special needs may refer to a child with specific physical, medical, mental, learning, or emotional disabilities or may be determined by factors such as age (school-aged children and teens), sibling status, race (in some states), and risk factors such as a family history of mental illness. Guidelines for classifying a child as having special needs vary by state, according to state statute." *(Source: Adopt.org glossary)*

• State license (page 131): All foster parents in the U.S. must be licensed or approved in order to provide care for children. The licensing process is different in each state. To find out your local rules and state requirements, visit AdoptUSKids.org/adoption-and-foster-care/how-to-adopt-and-foster/state-information

• Straight adoption: This is a term that many people in the adoption community try to avoid, as it can sound negative. But this is the same as adopting legally free children through Waiting Texas Children.

• Termination of parental rights (page 153): "The legal process that permanently severs a parent's rights to a child." *(Source: DaveThomasFoundation. org/adoption-guide/terms/)*

• Uniform Adoption Act (page 93): "A law that went in effect to try to make the adoption process more uniform. Birth mothers can change their mind about adoption until they sign the legal paperwork. Typically the birth mother has 48 to 72 hours after birth to change her mind. However, each state varies on the time frame they offer a birth mother to sign her paperwork. Some states even follow the Uniform Adoption Act allowing a mother up to eight days to change her mind." *(Source: Family-Law.FreeAdvice.com/family-law/adoption_law/reverse_adoption.htm)*

• USCIS (page 122): "Government agency that oversees lawful immigration to the United States." *(Source: Law.Cornell.edu/wex/united_states_citizenship_and_immigration_services_uscis)*

• Waiting Texas Children (legally free children) (pages 30, 98): "Children in the public child welfare system who cannot return to their birth homes and need permanent, loving families to help them grow up safe and secure." *(Source: AdoptiveFamilies.com/how-to-adopt/adoption-terms-glossary/)*

Adoption Process Overview

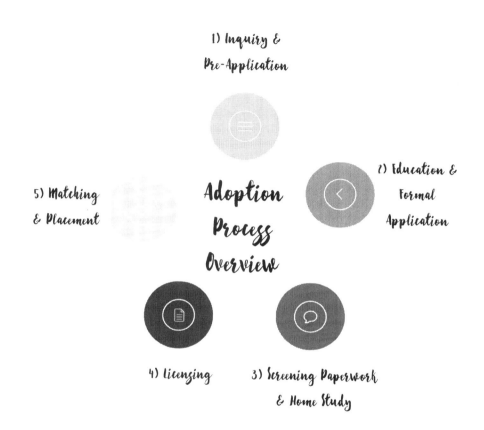

1) Inquiry &
Pre-Application

2) Education &
Formal
Application

Adoption
Process
Overview

5) Matching
& Placement

4) Licensing

3) Screening Paperwork
& Home Study

CPS Process, Rules and Regulations

And last but certainly not least, I wanted to share some helpful rules from DFPS that you may not be aware, but that are important to keep track of and note. There are a lot of stipulations, and you want to rely on your agency for a full and thorough list, but I wanted to give you a few that I reference throughout the book so that you can easily access them later. And as always, the rules can vary from state to state. So make sure you check with your state on their specifics.

Basic Foster Parent Requirements:

- Be at least 21 years of age, financially stable, responsible, and mature adult
- Complete an application (staff will assist you, if you prefer)
- Share information regarding your background and lifestyle
- Provide relative and non-relative references
- Show proof of marriage and/or divorce (if applicable)
- Agree to a home study, which includes visits with all household members
- Allow staff to complete a criminal history background check and an abuse/neglect check on all adults in the household
- Attend free training to learn about issues of abused and neglected children
- Have adequate sleeping space
- Allow no more than six children in the home including your own children or children for whom you provide day care
- Agree to a non-physical discipline policy

- Permit fire, health and safety inspections of the home

- Vaccinate all pets

- Obtain and maintain CPR/First Aid Certification

- Obtain TB testing as required by the local health department for household members

- Attend 20 hours or more of training each year

Spanking and Corporal Punishment

Spanking and corporal punishment is not allowed when a child is under DFPS conservatorship. This is for a variety of reasons, but primarily it has to do with the trauma and/or abuse that many of the children have experienced.

Corporal punishment is defined by DFPS as the infliction of physical pain on any part of a child's body as means of controlling or managing the child's behavior (40 TAC §749.1953). It includes:

- Hitting or spanking a child with a hand or instrument

- Forcing or requiring the child to do any of the following as a method of managing or controlling behavior:

- Performing any form of physical exercise, such as running laps or doing sit ups or pushups

- Holding a physical position, such as kneeling or squatting

- Doing any form of "unproductive work," defined as work that serves no purpose except to demean the child. Examples include moving rocks or logs from one pile to another or digging a hole and then filling it in.

• DFPS Rules, 40 TAC §749.1955 *(Source: DFPS.state.tx.us/handbooks/CPS/Files/*

CPS_pg_6400.asp)

Social Media

This is a difficult rule to keep and one you may forget, but you are not allowed to post your child's face online or on any social media sites while they are in DFPS care. You can, and are still encouraged, to get family pictures and can take pictures of events to keep track of your memories for their life book. The official rule in Texas states:

"No. Rules 748.1101 and 749.1003 require that you ensure the child's right to confidential care and treatment. Confidential care and treatment includes refraining from identifying a foster child or child in residential care as such in any internet communications with others, including social networking sites. Pictures or information identifying a child as a foster child or child in residential care on the Internet, including social networking sites, violates the child's right to confidential care." *(Source:*

DFPS.State.TX.US/Child_Care/Residential_Child_Care_Licensing/faqs_RCCL.asp)

Traveling Rules

Again, this varies by state so make sure you know your states laws, but you definitely need to know when and where you can and can't travel. DFPS encourages creating memories and family bonding, so you just want to make sure you do that in the correct capacity. There are separate rules for in-state and out-of-state travel.

<u>In-State Travel</u>

Type of Travel	Approval Required	CPS Staff Must
• Routine • Fewer than 48 hours away from facility or home	No	None
More than 72 hours with the caregiver, away from facility or home	Written approval by the caseworker or the caseworker's supervisor	• Determine the appropriateness of the travel • Provide written documentation, if the travel is approved
More than 48 hours with a person who is not a caregiver or relative	Written approval by the caseworker or the caseworker's supervisor	• Determine the appropriateness of the travel • Provide written documentation, if the travel is approved

(Source: DFPS.state.tx.us/handbooks/CPS/Files/CPS_pg_6400.asp#CPS_647)

Out-of-State Travel

Type of Travel	Approval Required	CPS Staff Must
Outside of State	• CPS approval • Notice to the court, or the courts written approval if the court that has jurisdiction over the case requires it, or both	• Determine the appropriateness of the travel • Notify the court about the plans to travel, or request court approval, as appropriate
Outside of the U.S.	• CPS review • Court approval	• Help the caregiver complete Form 2069 Caregiver Declaration Regarding Out-of-Country Travel; • Submit a petition to the court. • Document the reasons CPS opposes travel outside the U.S., when applicable

(Source: DFPS.state.tx.us/handbooks/CPS/Files/CPS_pg_6400.asp#CPS_647)

Babysitters, Caregivers, and Respite Care:

There are quite a few rules when it comes to having other people watching your foster child in the event that you need to go to a work event, take time with your spouse, go out of town, have daily care, etc. There are three types of providers:

216

- <u>Babysitters:</u> Someone who provides short-term or infrequent child care. They must always be deemed age-appropriate, mature, trustworthy individuals by the foster parents using their services.

  - Babysitters may babysit during the day or overnight, unless they are minors. Babysitters who are minors must limit the number of hours that they babysit and may not care for children overnight. See DFPS rules 7911.2 Minor Babysitters for more information.

  - CPS employees may not act as babysitters or provide overnight care for a child in foster care not related to them except as otherwise provided in policy when an appropriate placement is not available. See DFPS rules 4152.2 Meeting a Child's Needs Until a Placement Is Secured for more information.

  - Your agency case manager needs to be notified of baby-sitters that you plan on having as they must be documented, have passed a background check, be CPR-certified, and have their fingerprints run through the FBI agency database.

- <u>Caregivers:</u> Someone who regularly provides child care and supervision when the foster parent is unavailable. Note: Regularly is defined as at least four hours a day, three or more times a week for more than nine consecutive weeks. Examples of alternate caregivers include, but are not limited to:

- Adult household members who have responsibility as a caregiver for a foster child or an unrelated daycare provider

- Alternate caregivers, again, must be approved by your case manager. They must have a background check, have their finger prints ran by the FBI registry, and be CPR-certified, and they also must take the same pre-requisite classroom training you had to take as a foster parent. This obviously takes a little more work than the job of a babysitter.

- Licensed daycares, Mother's Day Out programs, and schools do not have to go through this process as they are already licensed by the State. However, you still have to notify your case manager of your plans to enroll them in these programs.

• <u>Respite care providers</u>: Those who go through the whole caregiver program to provide services to foster families who do not have alternate caregivers lined up.

Out-of-home respite care must be provided by:
- Registered or licensed day-care facilities
- Licensed or verified foster family homes or group homes
- Licensed or verified residential facilities that offer specialized care, such as camps, emergency shelters
- Programs specifically designed to provide respite care, such as respite care programs for families with children with disabilities, or Parents Night Out programs
- Individuals the adoptive parents have selected to provide respite care
- Programs for children that provide respite care to the adoptive parents while the child is participating in the program

In-home respite care must be provided by individuals who:
- Have been specifically trained to provide respite care to children with special needs, or
- Have been selected by the adoptive family to provide respite care and approved in the service plan for that purpose

Whether you have an alternative caregiver lined up or you will need respite care providers, I suggest you line these up early in case of an emergency. You never know when something could pop up and you may need help watching your child/children. You want to be prepared for that, if needed.

Personal Information

As a foster parent, you also want to protect your personal information from the birth family, especially if there are still visitations, and if you see them at family planning and court dates. You want to keep your last name, your address, where you work, and what part of town you live in confidential. Your case managers should not mention these items in the family planning meetings or court cases either and should protect your privacy. If there are meetings set up, they should be arranged at the CPS offices or at a neutral place. Talk to your agency about their rules on meeting and what they suggest.

Reporting

There is absolutely a LOT of reporting that has to be done on a daily, weekly, and monthly basis when you child is in DFPS care. You need to familiarize yourself with your agency's rules and your state's rules. These are just a few of the things you will be expected to keep track of:

- Medicine log

- Daily report

- Weekly report

- Incident report

(Source: DFPS.state.tx.us/child_care/residential_child_care_licensing/faqs_rccl.asp)

It's funny leaving this long list with you. Looking back at this now, I am thinking, man, I really hope no one is skimming the book and started here to get a feel for the process, because that would be so overwhelming! Hopefully after sharing our story and encouraging you, I have helped you feel empowered and not overwhelmed.

When I was traveling a lot for work, I was traveling for meetings, product launches, golf tournaments, and trade shows. Most of the time, I was in charge of planning and executing those events. The problem was that these events took place in all different locations in the U.S., most of which were nowhere near one of our offices so I couldn't just get something if I needed it. I would spend months preparing for these events, and I would pack for multiple scenarios, not always knowing exactly what I would need, if something would break, or if a customer would ask for a piece of literature I had not packed.

That is how adoption can feel at times. You don't really know which tools you may need along the way. So I want you to have something along your foster care and adoption adventure that you can come back to for quick reference when you hear these terms in your classes and more importantly when you start going through the process and experiencing this ride yourself.

Chapter 17:
My Closing Letter to You

Over three years ago, God called our family to something radical. Something that none of our friends and family had done. Something that we did not even know would change our life and our mission forever.

The call to domestic adoption through CPS changed our life, our family structure, and our purpose. It was not and is not always easy. It definitely was not always accepted or understood.

But God knew our son was just waiting to be a part of our family. And the day we got to meet him face-to-face for the first time was one of the top five moments in my life.

The adoption process—before, during, and after—will challenge you and your family in ways you never thought possible. I know it did for me.

But most of all, it permanently changed my relationship with God. I have NEVER relied on Him or trusted Him more. I only thought I loved God and showed His love before.

But that "experience," that path of adoption and reliance on God, has made me realize God's plan for my life and my family is intentional and so so so much better than even this Type A, party/event planner could have ever designed.

I am ready to move forward in reckless abandon for whatever God calls me to do. He has moved careers, money, our living situation, court dates, doctors, family members, you name it, for this one child to have a family. And if He has done all of this for our child already, why wouldn't He do all of these things in our life for whatever He calls us to do?

And, lucky for you, dear reader, I am writing this in the new year. The time of self-reflection for what we want for our new "New Year, New Me." I generally hate New Year's resolutions as I feel that they just make me look for my faults and realize that year-after-year I still fail to transform into this physically fit, healthy eating, June Cleaver mom.

So this year, in our small group, we were asked to come up with one word for our year—a goal or a mantra. I like this so much better because it is positive, and I plan on doing this for years to come.

This year my word, or words I should say as this wordy momma couldn't fit it all in just one word, is "trust boldly."

I don't know if it comes with the Type A territory, but "letting go" and "go with the flow" aren't my strong suits. I want a plan, a five-year plan, a back-up plan, and some detailed footnotes to go along with it.

But God has called into my life more than that. I feel like He has called me and my family to make some pretty bold (or what others may call crazy) changes. That stirring and that feeling all started with our first adoption.

It has also been such a huge blessing to be writing about our experiences from our first adoption and such amazing timing because we are now pursuing our second domestic CPS adoption. And I have to tell you, so many of those same old fears and anxieties have resurfaced. While this will be a whole new experience and a different time in our lives, it has been so amazing to be able to rehash all those "aha moments" with God and apply them to us going through this process all over again. So know, sweet friend, I am truly walking this path with you.

My prayer this year is that I can continue to trust God to make these drastic changes, go in bold directions, and accept His call no matter what. And I pray you do, too, and you can finally say "yes!" to a whole new story for you and your family.

xoxo

Holly Nicole James

About the Author

Holly Nicole James is a momma to two fun, energetic boys, and wife to her always supportive husband, Jeremy. Holly's dream to adopt began in junior high after learning about population control laws in China. It was a "must-accept" checklist item to move beyond dating, and her husband gladly accepted. After having their first son through pregnancy, Holly and Jeremy decided to next expand their family through domestic, CPS adoption.

After their youngest son joined their family, more and more people began asking questions about their process and adoption life. It was then that Holly saw the need for a spotlight to be shed on adoption, what it entails, and how to join alongside families who are adopting. She began advocating for adoption and sharing her story in March of 2016.

Holly has been featured in Buckner International's quarterly magazine, and her story has been shared on World Adoption Day and Stand for Life.

You can find her sharing more of her story of adoption through CPS and a glimpse into the everyday life of what adoption and motherhood can really look like on her website HollyNicoleJames.com.

holly nicole james

ADOPTION ADVOCATE

holly nicole james

"I LOVE ADOPTION
& HOW
**GOD'S
LOVE**
SHINES THROUGH IT."

*-Holly Nicole James,
Adoption Advocate*

Made in the USA
Middletown, DE
13 August 2017